EVERY DAY HEROES

TRUE STORIES

OF

SIMPLE GRACE AND COURAGE

BY KARMA YESHE DORJE

ISBN 978-0-615-51400-0

This book is dedicated to my two sons:

Raymond Churchfield III, whom I like to call My Son the Warrior. From him I have learned so much.

And

Kneil Wissel, whom I like to call My Son the Wizard. He has been so patient with me, even when others have not.

ACKNOWLEDGEMENTS

The heartful wisdom and unconditional love celebrated in this book first became visible to me in the person of my life partner, Gemini Black. Many years it took me, around her every day, to realize I was in the presence of something; and many years after that to see the ever-changing face of this same miracle in the every day heroes reported in this book. Then gradually after that, their stories began to find their way onto the paper. (Many times I have written about Gemini herself, but I have not yet scratched the surface.)

All of those every day heroes and surprise protagonists celebrated herein, all of those unconditional lovers and crazy lovers, are the true authors of this book, in all but the literary sense. All I did was write it down. They created it, and then the angels hit me over the heart enough to show me how to get it onto paper. Circumstances also have caused a delay in writing down the stories of many others equally great; and as the bumps and jiggles of the poetic life position them to me, their stories may yet be told in a similar medium.

I might first have mentioned my spiritual teachers, and many a more worthy student would have done so. I seem however to have wandered forth into this lifetime with more of a mission to learn passion than manners. With tremendous wisdom and love I have been taught nevertheless by, in chronological order, Jason Lotterhan in San Francisco, Colin Cole in Seattle, Shiela, Sister Ellie in Tulsa, and Jackie Roemer in Tulsa.

The angels and spirit entities, whom I call upon every time I sit down to fiddle with the keys, receive mention this far down in the list only because they already are well known for serving as muse to many others. They show up every time, demanding neither literary résumé from me nor credit for themselves. And to work with the likes of me through a project like this one, from beginning to end, obviously each one of them has a very good sense of humor, and patience beyond belief.

On the earthly side of things, inspiring me very much is an old friend, Anand Prahlad, whose name was Dennis Folly when he and I were doing carpentry together. Seeing him, I decided if I could write poetry half as well as he, I could publish this book.

Also inspiring my work, in their own way, are a different set of characters: all the women I loved and left, and all the women who loved me and left me. We entertain no coincidences here; and without these experiences, the sweet ones and the chastening ones, there could be no book resembling this one, from the typewriter of this person. (Whenever I have complained about any one of these, it has arisen from a terrible ignorance on my part, of the subtle purposes that run through our deeply felt experiences.) In fullness of time, maybe beyond the end of this lifetime, I will be smart enough, and sensitive enough, to get together with each one of them in turn, to celebrate the sweet things and to laugh at myself very much.

A special mention here for Nick Guy, my supervisor when I worked with developmentally disabled folks in Seattle. It was he who told me that he let me work with clients a little more independently than he might have, because I am passionate about my work. Remembering that remark has cheered me when nothing else did.

I am deeply indebted to Michael Daniels, editor and designer of books I contributed to in the past, who advised me and encouraged me during the hardest parts of getting this book to press; to Alice Ducharme, who was very patient and supportive in the early stages of getting this book ready; to Mary Ann VanHoomissen, who typed in most of the manuscript; to Eileen Windstrom, skilled and accurate and very patient, who finished the typing in, and handled the designing process as if it were easy; and to Judith Hill, an old friend who encouraged me when I needed it most.

KYD

26 Jan. and 27 Feb. 2008

Tulsa

HEROES AT THE FRONT

Jean-Marie is shown on the front cover, riding to the ticket counter on a baggage cart, at Juscelino Kubitschek Airport, in Brasilia, on the day described in Silence of a poet, p.225. The author stopped pushing just long enough to take the picture.

Hara, every day hero of the poem by the same name, p.29, is seen in a quiet moment on the inside front cover.

PREFACE

I am a mere poet. It is given to me only to write about the great ones I see around me in every day life.

Sometimes their sensitivity is so great that they have been awarded a mental health diagnosis. Sometimes they are attempting by their simplicity to reflect the love of God, and so have left a part of the intellect back home on the other side of the veil. Sometimes they are developing strength and courage, or even teaching those qualities, by going about in a body which is disabled.

And there must be yet a fourth category of entrée to everyday greatness, pertaining to the many, otherwise unlabeled heroes depicted here. Call it for now the daemon which would not leave Socrates alone.

A few animals will show up here also as heroes and protagonists. There would be more of them, if I would learn to notice them better. They have allowed us to underestimate them for a very long time.

Grace has placed me unawares in the path of these great ones one after another, for many years, by allowing me to be ill-suited somehow to do much else but to work in and around the disabled community. I do things slowly, and this is not well tolerated in most lines of work. But as my thinking has become unable somehow to keep very well to the mainstream, my disabled sisters and brothers in their mercy seem to have taken me more and more as their own. And there I have been, to watch and to write.

<u>These poems are true stories</u>, as true as poetic locution permits. I can only swear to you that this is so. The only caveat to this concerns several that took place where the five senses don't go, and so would not lend themselves to certain conventional rules of proof.

Some of my poems chronicle the overt heroism and grace which come before me to be told. Others are included for characterization of this wonderful Earth and her family — a milieu of paradox and mystery behind which every day heroes and crazy lovers hide, like the leaves in a forest.

By my own faculties I am neither writer nor poet. But when I sit in front of the tablet, sometimes I remember first to hold the pen in both hands prayerfully above the head. After that it seems to run by itself. I don't know how it does that.

There will be found, on the other hand, errors and mistaken ideas in this book, and I am the author of those.

Some of the names have been changed, a few have not been changed, and some have been omitted.

KYD

6 and 8 March 2006

Casa de Dom Inacio, Brasil

A WORD ABOUT CYCLES

Everything goes in cycles, right? Well so do I.

Terrible times and wonderful times follow each other in succession, as the day follows the night. Goofy poems and heartbreaking poems come in pairs. Poems that inspire and poems that make me laugh all flow through these old hands, in no predictable sequence of linear time.

Cycles, as distinguished in the lives and works of famous poets, often look suspiciously like they were identified and characterized a hundred years later by someone writing a thesis. Like the poet had been in a certain sort of mood for 10 or 20 years, and all of her/his poems from that "cycle" may be analyzed through the lens of that. Then another long epoch in the life, a brand new mood, and a different flavor sensible to the scholars.

Okay, well I go through really long, slow changes like that too. I can validate that. In my core, one foolishness follows another – each digging in for a tragically long time, then giving way in a flash to another one, equally challenging but more rewarding.

But wherever my poems come from, the ones in this book, there's a whole different way of telling time there. Cycles, as I think of them, turn over quickly, back and forth, from one to another. I am accustomed to seeing where one leaves off and another begins with no more objectivity than that with which the doctors can tell diseases apart. But with things that I take rather to heart, my poems and my diseases for example, still I do my own classifying.

So it is that, as best I can, I have classified my poetry in this book into my kind of cycles. To do so, I look generally at the sort of characters in them. The classification as to cycle appears at the beginning of each poem, and also in abbreviated form after each title in the Table of Contents.

KEY TO THE CYCLES

Every Day Heroes (EDH) are seemingly ordinary folks (humans or occasionally animals) who step up and do a wonderful, big-hearted or very brave act, when one is needed. Crazy Love (CL) can refer to the actions of a similar bunch, but generally with strong feelings shown, and seeming to fail some fundamental test of reason.

Those background events and characters in the Wide Weird Wonderful World (WWWW) poems are lending themselves body and soul to the manifestation of this world, where heroism and love play out. Goofy Poet (GP) poems can be similar to these, but emphasize an opportunity for the poet to learn some common sense – whether I actually learned it or not.

Poems in the Self Disclosure (SD) cycle are offered in a spirit of confession, and it scares the ego out of me to write them.

No explanation is offered for the couple of poems that are left unclassified (UNCL), except to say that it is intentional.

KYD

16 June 2010

On Amtrak in California

TABLE OF CONTENTS

CASA NOTE

Seventeen of the fifty seven true stories told in this book took place at the Casa de Dom Inacio (House of Saint Ignatius), in Abadiania, Goias, Brazil.

They can be found on pages 1, 29, 82, 91, 149, 155, 160, 165, 170, 173, 181, 185, 193, 198, 203, 219 and 225.

More information about the "Casa" can be found at the following websites:

www.AbadianiaPortal.com

www.AbadianiaTalesandTravel.com

The Whistle Blower

WHISTLE BLOWER

A true story.
Time and place: Abadiania, Brasil
                  July and August, 2007
Crazy Love Cycle

Is she mad? She doesn't even know
What operation she's having,"
Said one spirit entity to another,
Laughing as she passed by in a trance.

"They didn't think I could hear them,"
She said, grinning slightly.
"But I have to be able to.
 I'm a spiritual whistle blower,"

The first time I saw her,
She was waiting in line
At a mighty healing center.

The tiny kitten she was holding
Had peed in her hair
During the night, she said.

Now she held him
And blew gently on his head.
Of her own life force
She seemed to give him

In ways seldom seen
Among mothers with their babies,
She attended that day
To this orphaned kitten.

In the collar of her jersey
She nestled him by her larynx –
Bathing him in teachings
All souls need to hear.

I watched for her
After that day in the line.
Could she keep that five day old kitten alive?
Could she handle it if he died?

Great love has its price –
As I had seen already
In the lives of others.

We need all the whistle blowers
We can get,

So in my conceit I prepared myself,
To keep an eye on this one
In her cycle of despair.

Four days I watched,
And then she appeared.

Yes, the cat had died.
No, she was fine.

Two days he lay in state,
She told me.
Then she buried him
With all due ritual,
And planted a flower on the grave.

Later on she told me stories
That strained on all my belief –

Of grand plans for our aching planet,
And the part that she would play.

But then I would remember
That day with the cat –
And there was nothing in me
That could label her deluded.

So now, in the little spiritual etiquette that I know,
I will believe anything that she says,
But confess that
I cannot understand half of it.

And often I have wanted to tell her
Of this confidence placed,
And the struggle that attends it.

But she never stops talking.

KYD
4 Aug 2007
Abadiania, Brasil

JACK'S CONVERSION

A true story.
Time and place: Bisbee, Arizona, 1996
Wide, Weird, Wonderful World Cycle

Jack and his brother were ringleaders.

One Arizona Summer,
Followed along by a couple of little guys,
They made a lot of mischief.
Terrorized many small animals.

One time the two stayed out all night.
'Next day we found jack's brother dead.

Rumor had it the cat they bothered that night
Turned out to be a mountain lion cub.

Jack stayed by his brother's body that morning.
No one could persuade him to leave.

When the body was hauled away
Jack followed the vehicle.

Down the street and around the corner,
He ran 'til he was out of sight.

Jack came back later,
More tired than we had ever seen him,
His eyes a vacant stare.

Jack moped around all that summer.
'Didn't want to play.

Certainly stayed out of mischief.
Tormented no more animals.

My neighbor was a quiet man.
Very often that year Jack would come to his door.
He would go inside and sit silently
For long periods of time.

One day, passing my neighbor's house,
I saw Jack on the porch;
Sad eyes,
Shoulders slumped.

Jack shrank from me when I approached.
But I went to him and apologized.

Once earlier on, in my exasperation,
I had thrown a stone at Jack and his gang.

Now I told him
I saw him in an entirely new light
And would like to be his friend,
 If he would let me.

He let me come up to him
And put my hand on his shoulder.

We sat that way for a couple minutes,
Then Jack walked off.

It would take a little more time for Jack and me.
And words were not enough.

You see,
Jack was a dog.

KYD
19 April 2004
El Pauji, Venezuela

BEAR MAN

A true story.
Time and place: A small town in Pennsylvania
                  April or May, 2006
Every Day Heroes Cycle

Lee had heard of those bear traps
His neighbors in that rural area were setting.

Now, on an early morning walk with his dog,
He looked into a neighbor's yard
And there he saw one!

A big, imposing thing it was,
Made of solid steel culvert pipe.
Cold and hard as the intent of the owner.

Curious as he always was,
Lee leashed his dog to that neighbor's mailbox
And walked in for a closer look.

Only then did he see
The two bear cubs,
Just across the yard.

He looked at the trap again,
Saw that the door was sprung shut,
And a horrible realization formed.

Peeking in through the tiny air holes
In that giant trap,
Lee confirmed the terrible thought:

Mama bear was trapped inside,
Her cubs were unprotected,
And whoever dared to open that door
Would be right between them!

Well, Lee is a plain spoken
And plain thinking guy.

He knew the rules out there:
You can't shoot the bears.
But you can trap them
And take them for a long ride.

So imagine the grief of that mother:
Trapped, then hauled away, helpless,
Her babies standing by —
Never to see her again,
Sure to perish miserably without her.

So what would you do
If you were that mother bear,
After an experience like that?

How would you treat the next humans you met?

And how would the intent
Of the wilderness management rules be served,
If a passive-aggressive killing
Of two bear cubs were not prevented?

Quicker done than told,
Lee opened that steel monstrosity,
And the bear never did eat him!

The real danger to Lee came
From the house-holder/bear-trapper.

Remember Lee's dog, leashed to the mailbox?
Well, a very big dog he was,
And filled with common sense
Not learned from Lee.

Seeing Lee's wonderful and compassionate
Flirtation with disaster,

The dog very prudently pulled the mailbox
Loose from the ground,
And ran home dragging it.

Needless to say
This woke the owner of the trap.

He looked out the window,
And Lee was busted.

A crime of conscience it was,
And probably cost him about a grand.

My cousin helped to pay the fine.

KYD
23 May 2006
Stewartsville

WARNING

A true story with a bit of interpretation.
Time and place: On our porch in Tulsa
                          Probably 2006
Every Day Heroes Cycle

"Hey, stay out of there.
It's not safe!"

It was a neighborhood raccoon
She was warning,
As she reached through the top of the trap
And poked at him.

Joe the raccoon backed out of the trap,
And came around for a closer look
At this clown-faced cat.

He was only a raccoon however,
And he couldn't quite make out
What she was saying.

Back he went to the cat chow,
In that funny-looking structure.

"Hey, this is serious!"
She reached through the air hole again
Poked him, looked through again,
And poked him another time.

Chelsea had seen what happens
To raccoons, even to unfriendly cats,
If they go in there.

She was over a year old now,
And she knew.

Gemini, one of the humans, pulls the cord,
The door drops shut,
And both the humans
Take that animal for a long ride.

They even told her
That they never hurt anyone –
They just drop them off across the river.

But they never find their way back!
And Chelsea had no problem
With poor old Joe.

He just came to eat Yeshe's cat chow.
Never bothered anybody.

She even kind of liked the old boy –
And now he was in danger
Of going for that long ride!

A second time he came out
To see what was the matter.

And a third time too.
Now he even came over and sniffed her,
To try to understand
What she was telling him.

Then he went back into that trap.
What could she do!
Didn't the humans understand
That Yeshe could just
Buy more of that cat chow?

Freedom is so important, you know —
And Joe was about to lose a bit of his.

She poked and poked
And looked through that hole
Then poked some more.

But dear old Joe —
She hadn't even felt much for him 'til now —
He never did understand her warning.

He went all the way in
To the cat chow this time.

And "pop!"
Down came the door.

Gemini had pulled the cord,
And trapped old Joe.

It really happened.
Nothing she tried had worked.

                        KYD
                        19 Sep 2007
                        Tulsa

DOCTOR HECTOR

A true story.
Time and place: Tacoma, Washington
                  23 December 2007
Every Day Heroes Cycle

Hector's status in the house
Seemed a little lower than the other cat.
Tom number two he was.

Aloisius, the hero of some past turmoil
Among the humans in the house,
Ate no better than Hector.

Both had the run of the house.
Both were gently loved
By the humans there.

Except for the children of course,
Who loved to tug on kitties.

Aloisius distinguished himself over time,
By allowing little children
To carry him under one arm –
But only briefly.

With regal bearing
Aloisius got right into the mix,
With three pushy dogs in the house.

Hector was more in the background –
Under chairs and such – but
Still he was equally friendly to me.

My first three nights as houseguest,
Sleeping on the sofa, the two alternated
Sleeping on top of me.

One purred as loudly as the other,
Neither could force the other off,
And so it went.

It seemed to make little difference
Which one watched with me
On any particular hour.

Until the fourth night, that is.

Running long and hard that day
On my family Christmas visits,
I woke up at midnight
With a nasty sore throat.

Swallowing in pain,
I planned my trusted remedies:

"Tomorrow I'll find some vitamin C.
That'll fix it!"

Time passed.
Too uncomfortable to sleep.
Too comfortable to get up.

<u>Then came Hector</u>.
Across the coffee table,
Into his customary position on my chest.

But this time
A little paw reached out.
Right to the spot that hurt —
Near the Adam's apple I believe.

He pushed hard,
And locked into his position.

Neither of us moved.

A bit of a healing student myself –
'Though not on Hector's level –
I knew right away
He was into something.

There I lay, little paw in my neck,
And marveled as the pain went away!

For half an hour he worked,
Then hopped down and walked away –
Same as any other night
You might have thought.

But the pain was gone.
And it stayed gone.

Later he meowed,
And I got up
And let him out as usual.

That's my friend, Doctor Hector.
Isn't there anything else
I can do for you, Doc?

KYD
24 December 2007
Sea Tac, Washington

FOOLERY

A true story.
Time and place: On a long car ride in Costa Rica
                  2004
Crazy Love Cycle

"I'd like to become a saint," he said,
"And I figure a way to do it
Is to give people what they want."

The mind reeled at such an idea.

It was certainly a noble aspiration,
And George would be far from the first to try.

Besides that, I believe he had
A system that may actually work.

Some will be well served, straight up,
By getting what they want.

Others, maybe quite a few,
Will learn to regret their wish —
And so increase in wisdom very much.

I believe he was sincere and not a con.
I had met him that day
In the company of my friend,
For whom he was doing a selfless act.

Nor was he seeking approval,
Because the way that he said it,
It was sure to be disbelieved by most.

A few years earlier I had heard
A simple way to avoid being noticed –
If you happen to be an outrageous person:

Just tell the truth!
People won't believe you anyway.

I think George understood this very well;
And when someone called attention
To his act of kindness that day,

It was very simple for him
Just to be taken for a fool.

Go for it, George!

                    KYD
                    27 February 2006
                    Casa de Dom Inacio, Brasil

LESSON PLAN FOR AN ANGEL

A true story.
Time and place: West coast of U.S.
                 Especially around Berkeley
                 Approx. 1979 to 1987
Crazy Love Cycle

I met you when you applied
To work in my department

And I caused you to be
Turned down in favor of another.

I caught up to you to apologize,
Citing justice for a faithful worker.

You excused it as if
Nothing had happened,
And soon became my friend.

Teach me to forgive perfectly
And without hesitation.

You turned down my proposal
Because of an agenda of mercy
That I knew nothing of,
Which kept you from being with me.

And later when I said
The proposal was no more

You grabbed me
And ripped my shirt –

The only anger I ever saw
In eight years as your friend.

And only much later,
Long after your death in fact,
Did I begin to unravel
The story behind it all.

Teach me when love reaches passion
Even then to do the math,
And to show up where I'm needed most –

Nor even to take credit later
For duty of a stunning sort
When even to tell the story
Would compromise the act itself.

Living later near a sailboat harbor
On a tiny, rural island,

The children loved you so
That they visited you each day.

You invited them for dinner once
And prepared with such love for the meal —

But seasoned with a lot of spice
Because your own defects of body
Had stripped you of the sense;

Then cried and told me later
That only one had eaten,
Having lived in Mexico for a bit.

Teach me to honor
Even those least in power,

As if the queen
Had come to call.

You said little of your disabilities,
And only by my diligence
Ever did I find them out.

Unable to hold a job,
Your work was calling on friends
With the gentleness of your love.

Unable to ride the trains,
Sensitive as you were to the air —

Unable to tie your shoes,
A hand and foot deformed since birth —

You limped over a small mountain
On most of your days,

With shoes untied
And friends to see.

Teach me the courage to notice
Only what needs to be done,
And not to count the cost.

You met a man
Kind and gentle in the extreme,
Whom the children followed also.

But his wife treated him badly
And that was too much for you.

Unable to drive due to seizures,
You begged for rides to his block —

And sat across from his house, knowing
He would leave her and come to you.

Not even I believed it
As I drove you there one day –

Yet soon it had come to pass,
And you and he were married
On a footbridge near my house

And you loved him til your death,
Telling always of his way with the kids.

Now teach me to know
How love conquers all,

That nothing else needs to matter,
And to march through any day.

KYD
28 August 2010
Abadiania

FORGIVENESS

This is a true story, best suited perhaps for reading
by those who happen to believe in reincarnation.
Time and place: Recife, Brasil
                24 June 2004, 12:21 p.m.,
                +/- 2 minutes
Wide, Weird, Wonderful World Cycle

That was a mighty big gun you were carrying
The other day when you tried to hold me up.

Of course you and I had had
Dream time conversations about this
In the previous week or two.

You know, it's a good thing
I remembered a bit of those dreams.
Otherwise I might not have known what to do.

I really couldn't give you
My money and my passport that day.

It would have shut down
A couple of missions I am on,
Which could be worth about as much
As the rest of my life put together.

So already the odds in walking away from you
Began to look surprisingly good.

But ultimately
When I saw that gun
And you pulled on my arm,

The only thing to do
Was to trust the angels
Who sponsored those nocturnal conversations.

The angels who coached me to ask you
In your dream state
If you know what they do
To people who shoot tourists.

The angels who take responsibility
For the stuff they get me into.

Well, I walked away.
And you retreated into your deserted street.

And you know, when I followed the plan,
Those angels did their job so well

That when I noticed myself a couple minutes later:
I wasn't trembling.
I wasn't breathing hard.
None of that.

So now, what will you do?
Will you look for me in another lifetime?

I'll bet you won't.

I think when I walked away,
And you put away your gun;
That was forgiveness.

> KYD
> 4 July 2004
> Abadiania, Brasil

Alive and well, forgiven too

HARA

A true story.
Time and place: A street near the Casa de
                 Dom Inacio
                 January 2011
Every Day Heroes Cycle

"Why is Mario on a leash?" she demanded.
"He has a right to be free!"

I'd never seen her speak like that —
Never anything but gentle and agreeable.

So I sat down on the curb to watch.

Would this soft and gentle one
Really confront the woman walking the dog?

Mario was a very gentle little dog
Nearly as enlightened as
The human sponsor he lives with —

So the two of them
Had my attention always.

I was walking along actually
To observe their little intervention
On another friend of mine.

The sponsor, you see,
Would let my other friend
Take walks with Mario
On that otherwise useless leash:

She with perfect posture then,
Looking straight ahead,
Holding the leash a bit aloft;

While gently her little friend followed
Foregoing all he might have sniffed –
Though puzzled by the drill.

I spoke encouragement to the dog
Admiring his wise and healing ways;

For the one who led him now,
As even I could see,

Had gotten through childhood
Only by walking just right!

So who would prevail
I was waiting that day to see –

Would they both walk just so
At the end of the stroll,
As she'd been direly taught?

Or dart and wander
And see so much more –
As any dog knows to do?

And so enjoying each moment,
In sweet anticipation
Of which could prevail,

I gloated now to myself
As Hara came into view,

On how well this sensitive one
Would appreciate later on

My account of the intervention –
In early stage just then –

By Mario and his kind sponsor
And the angels who walked along!

Grinning quietly now
I greeted her as she came;

But her greeting was not a mild one!
Nor even addressed to me.

"Why is Mario on a leash?!"

She stood now directly in the way.

Then quickly came forward
And took the darn thing off.

Then she walked quietly away
And Mario did the same,

Both to the cafe nearby
Where the sponsor still hung out –

Leaving me to ponder this
For a day or two I think.

And only then to tell her
How few it is I've seen

Who can bring their kindness
With them wherever they go,

Yet keep somewhere the mindfulness
And the courage that it takes

To stand up to oppression
When it's right up in their face.

In this town where I met her
There's surprises all the time,

And anyone can be my teacher
If I'm conscious enough to watch.

    KYD
    17 Jan. 2011
    Abadiania

Hara

DRIVING WITH RALPH

A true story.
Time and place: En route, Princeton to Drew
                  University, Approximately 1968
Wide, Weird, Wonderful World Cycle

"We said we'd get someone with a car
To pick up Ralph Nader from Princeton,
And bring him here to speak,"
Said a student at the next table.

I eavesdropped a bit more,
As the two undergraduates described
Their obviously sensitive mission,
To friends in the snack bar.

"These two may not know the first thing
About Ralph Nader's famous research,"
I said to myself conspiratorially.

"They look a little naive," I thought.
"This could be my chance
For a glorious prank."

"We can't pay you anything but mileage,"
They said, when I offered to pick him up.

"That's okay," I said.
"I always wanted to meet Ralph Nader."

I wasn't telling them anything
They didn't need to know.

A few days later, at the appointed time,
I met the two of them
At our campus parking lot.

I watched their faces closely
As I led them to my Volkswagen bus.

No reaction! Not a trace.
Neither one had a clue, that
This was the terrible monster
So reviled by Nader.

In a front end crash
Nothing tested as poorly
As my dear old VW bus!

Good old Ralph, bless his heart,
Probably saved hundreds of lives –
By getting the beast outlawed
Within a few years.

He was famous already
For his position on this van.
Now I wanted to see –
What would be his position <u>in</u> this van?

You guessed it — and so did I!
Ralph sat right in the middle
When we picked him up —
Second seat of three.

He said nothing about our dreadful selection,
And my two patsies chattered happily —
Plying Mr. Nader with questions,
All the way back to our campus.

Quickly I parked and rushed to the auditorium —
Knowing Ralph was sure
To say something about his ride.

He had been late meeting us
At his office in Princeton,
And now his apology brought down the house:

 "I'm very sorry to be late," he said.
"So let's get started —
Now that I've arrived by Volkswagen bus."

Clever fellow that Ralph.
It was my prank,
And he got the laugh.

KYD
2 July 2007
Abadiania, Brasil

THEN CAME PETRONELA

A true story.
Time and place: Indonesia, on the government
                              steamers, 1991
Every Day Heroes Cycle

Those government steamers sure are great stuff.

Traveling from island to island to island,
They're the cheapest ride in Indonesia.
I didn't even mind waiting a day or so at the dock.

Outbound, I discovered the top deck —
Two days hanging out
With all the smokestacks and Europeans.

"It's funny the Indonesians don't come up here,"
I thought. "Must not appreciate the sunshine."
Worst I ever got was rained on.

Well, the local flu slowed me down
Just in time to get to know Petronela,
At her uncle's funky, little losmen.

My good fortune held, and two weeks later
I was returning with Petronela,
On the same or a similar ship.

She had ridden these ships before,
But it took me to introduce her
To the uppermost deck.

Evidently Indonesians put up with a lot
From government officials –
Including the officers of these ships.

And here's why I think that:

Petronela, hanging around
Her Uncle Johannes' losmen,
Never met a European she didn't like –
Perhaps because she had some attitudes
In common with them.

Well, Petronela liked that top deck immediately –
With all the white faces and backpacks.

And she had cousins in every port –
That's another thing about Petronela.

So shortly after we set sail
She said she was going below,
To bring some of them up to this wonderful deck.

Happily I concentrated on the seagulls,
'Til suddenly I heard a commotion
At the stairs leading from below.

I was slow to respond
And when I got there it was over.

Returning with her friends and relations,
Petronela, it seems, met an officer.

"You can't go up there," he said.

"Yes we can," she answered gamely.
She already knew half the people up there,
And when they flocked to the edge
To see what was the matter –

Guess what:
They shouted that old officer down.

The story went around the ship
At the speed of a seagull, it seems –

Because 20 minutes later
That top deck was full of Indonesians.

Big ones, little ones,
Fat ones, skinny ones.

Well, I wanted to interview a bunch of them –
With my faithful translator Petronela:

How had that segregation been enforced?

Did they know that so many other countries
Were kicking out that sort of crap?

Did they think the change would last?
Or would it be segregation as usual
On the very next voyage?

A veritable praxis it was,
In cultural anthropological investigation!

But it was not to be.

We went ashore "briefly" at the very next port,
For Petronella to lead some folks
To this great losmen,
Operated by relatives of hers.

And when we got back to the dock
We had missed the boat.

> KYD
> 22 May 2007
> Tulsa

HEART OF A PEMONE

A true story.
Time and place: Gran Sabana, Venezuela
                  2004
Every Day Heroes Cycle

Roberto used to guide the tourists
Coming off the ships in Caracas.
The money was very good.

But soon he quit that job,
And began offering ecotours
Way down south in the Gran Sabana –
Nearly on the Brazilian border.

In his little 4-wheel-drive he took four of us
To environmental sites and cultural sites.
At night we stayed at Pemone villages.
And in the daytime we swam a lot –
In places probably free of Anacondas.

Living as traditionally as they could,
Many of those indigenous folks
Depended on Roberto.

Wherever we stopped,
Roberto was the delivery guy.
He picked up handcrafted things to sell in town;
And he dropped off purchases
He had made for them.

"Roberto," I wrote,
In the guests' book in his office,
"Has the heart of a Pemone,
And the mind of an encyclopedia."

Not only that but Roberto's map,
Of UFO sightings in the Gran Sabana,
Sells in several stores in Santa Elena.

    KYD
    1 July 2007
    Casa de Dom Inacio, Brasil

EL ALTAR
(THE ALTAR)

A true story.
Time and place: El Pauji and thereabouts,
                    Venezuela, 2004
Wide, Weird, Wonderful World Cycle

"See that mountain over there," he said.
"It's called El Altar,
And whoever climbs to the top
Will have their third eye opened."

That sounded real good to me.
And Paulista came well recommended.

A traditional healer in Costa Rica
Had said to be sure to see Paulista.
"He's in one of those villages near Santa Elena."

And later, pausing in Santa Elena,
I heard of the same guy from Roberto,
The magical, mystical tour guide.

"He and his wife are 60 kilometers
Down that gravel road,
In a village started by hippies."

Now Paulista directed me
Farther down that gravel road —
But with no jitneys to take me there.

Then you turn left at an unmarked "road,"
Cross a creek, and follow a trail —
All the way up the mountain.

Now think about this:
To open the third eye!
A rare and precious gift.

I had met people who could really see.
Often they seemed to have been born that way.

I wanted that gift so badly!
There was so much I could do then.
I believed I could have it in the next lifetime —
But maybe I would not have to wait!

"You can walk there in one day,
And back the next," he said.
"I think there is even lodging
At the bottom of the mountain."

First came the rainstorm.

A bit of mercy from the angels
Throughout my life,
In the face of all the challenges
And adversities I have given myself,
Has been that I seldom get rained on.

Today, then, was marked as a very special day!
About an hour down the road,
It rained so hard that I could hardly see to walk.

No place to take shelter –
But I gave thanks for the rain.

Now the angels would see me
Marching right along –
And would know that I really wanted this!

Okay, so who sent that big truck
Speeding along,
Chasing me off the road
Into a big puddle?

Well, never mind.
Chalk it up –
Test number two.
Just keep walking,
Everything will dry.

Now is this the turnoff he spoke of?
'No way to know.
Better to stay on the road
'Til I meet someone to ask.

Down the road I knocked on a door.
My informant, in his very regional Spanish,
Seemed to be saying yes,
That was the road back there.
Boy did he think I was nuts!

Out there in gold-mining country, however,
There is no safety Gestapo
To keep you from "endangering yourself."

Back up the road, around the corner —
And onto a road that soon disappeared.

There were three small, rustic houses,
Scattered along a hillside —
Which by gravity eventually
Urged me to the creek at the bottom.

Oh, the creek!
Yes, but where was the trail at the other side?

No one in sight. But eventually –
By walking much too close
To those miners' cabins –
I found some stones in the creek,
With a trace of a trail opposite.

I was at the rim of the Amazon Basin, mind you –
Well within Anaconda territory.

Anaconda, I had been hearing,
Like to wait for lunch to come along.

This was all hearsay to me,
But they seem to prefer waiting in still water.
Dropping from a tree will do, however.

What other tricks they may fancy
Had not been told to me yet.
Just ahead of me, for example,
Lay tall grass with a trace of a very narrow trail.

Soaked from the rain,
The grass leaned into the trail,
Meeting in the middle, so that –

Yes, you could probably follow the trail.
No, you could not see the next step ahead of you.

Right ahead of me,
Seen more clearly than from Paulista's house –
But not seeming to be much closer –
I gazed on El Altar.

And in my heart
I gazed also on people that I love,
And plans that I love.

I had been a careless father,
Then sobered up
When my sons were grown.

Somehow I must make it up to them.
And I hadn't even figured out
How to do that yet.

Then there was the woman I love:
Fiercely independent all her life.
Soon to be diagnosed obsessive-compulsive.
Also showing signs of a physical disease
That will make her depend on someone.

A risk-taker all my life,
Nothing had persuaded me to change –

Until the picture came to mind
A couple years before, of Gemini,
That partner of mine:

Incarcerated helpless in a nursing home.
Directed about by control types –
No place there for her rituals
Of decontamination and order.

I looked at my terrible trade off then.

To plunge ahead and maybe come back
With this huge gift:

A wonderful blessing to all around me –
If I managed to use it well.

To plunge ahead and maybe come back. . .
Not at all:
To watch helpless from somewhere else
As my work went undone.

I turned back then.
The thought of that was too much for me.

El Altar, The Altar,
I have written you very large
In my book of unfinished business.

I will come to you again,
Better prepared
To pay the proper price.

                    KYD
                    3 and 4 July 2007
                    Abadiania, Brasil

BRIAN WILLSON DID IT

A true story.
Time and place: Concord military supply depot,
                  California, Nineteen eighties
Every Day Heroes Cycle
Note: This is a different Brian Willson, not a member of a
well-known musical group.

Brian Willson stood in front of a train.
Yes he did.

Next day
Everyone in the Bay Area
Knew his name.

The munitions train didn't stop.

Brian Willson lost his legs;
But not his love.

No anger or resentment
In the newspaper interviews.

He was a spokesman now.
The Bay Area listened,
And the peace and love came through.

Soon a local priest,
Arguing with The Vatican,
Was told he might as well
Stand in front of a train.

Yes, he said,
But Brian Willson did it!

                     KYD
                     4 June, 2005
                     Walker Hall, Tulsa

MARY:
The Wonderful Logic of a No-Account Hero

A true story.
Time and place: A transitional housing shelter
                 2005
Every Day Heroes Cycle

"He protected me from you,
Now I'll protect you from him."

So saying, Mary took up her position,
Next to Cynthia on the living room couch.

Recently paroled to the shelter where I worked,
Mary irritated nearly everyone –
But in such a wonderful variety of ways.

No pretension was safe
When Mary was around.

"He protected me from you,
Now I'll protect you from him."

Mary volunteered for the task
About the same moment that I picked her for it.

"You stay with her," I said.
"I'll go out back and talk with Mike."

Cynthia had just seen Mike
Finish a fight he did not start.

Mike, another con, wasn't good at calming down.
He came home, went to the back yard,
And told his friends
He was sure to go back to jail now.

Cynthia had freaked out, run home,
And called the cops.
Now she was sure Mike would start on her next.

"He protected me from you,
Now I'll protect you from him."

In the goes-around-comes-around of street life
This was all goofy and backwards, of course –
And I knew it was exactly what Mary would do.

Mary wasn't good for much –
Unless you took a closer look.

She didn't do house chores.
She didn't do pleasantries.
Mary was only there for the big plays.

A week earlier she had provoked Cynthia at dinner.
Cynthia, big strong woman,
Chased Mary into the kitchen.
Mike got between them before I could.

"He protected me from you," Mary says,
"Now I'll protect you from him."

KYD, 5 October 2005

EMILY

A true story.
Time and place: Tulsa
                  23 May 2010
Wide, Weird, Wonderful World Cycle

"When I saw that ring
All I could think to say was YES!"
 She said —

Demonstrating for her laughing girlfriends
Just how she supposedly lunged
For the prize.

 "I knew I didn't love him,
But I thought he was my last chance ever,
To get married and raise a family."

Hanging out after our recovery group,
Her other two listeners
Both were women.

Just for an instant I wondered:
 "Is this funny?"

It was ,of course,
And in that very poignant way
That makes you laugh
A little bit too loud.

I, not a member of their sex,
Had no experience
Of waiting to be asked —

Not to the prom.
Not to my wedding day.

I had been no smarter
Than this fair maid --
And tragically shy
When it mattered most.

Yet I had had my choice —
Stepping up
And asking straight away.

No waiting about
As the years passed.

You can step up the pace
Of your asking, and
Of the searching that you do —

But how do you wait a little harder?
What's a good logistic for that?

Famous they are,
Infamous even, these women,
For their intuition!

So where did they learn it –
The subtleties of their kind?

This ain't rocket science now.

I never was any good even
At doing the chasing part.

But I knew after that evening
From what it is
They learn their craft.

If you can learn to wait a little harder,
What is there left
You could not learn to do?

                KYD
                31 May 2010
                Tulsa

SHORT BUS

A true story.
Time and place: On a special education
                  school bus, In recent years
Every Day Heroes Cycle

Little Eddie's mother often had to drag him
Onto the bus
Kicking and screaming,
Spitting on anyone he could.

Other days he would walk on peacefully –
Then begin to spit
After he was strapped into the seat.

He was a dead shot at two seats away.
Children in front of him tended to wear a hood.

Democratic at heart,
Eddie took an equal interest
In spitting on the drivers.

We kept a seat vacant behind him,
And reached around from there to strap him in.

We asked to relocate a seat
All the way to the back of the bus,
To keep Eddie out of range.
But safety regulations did not allow it.

Morale was low on the bus.
Kids were slow coming out from the school.
We would threaten to leave
Without one or another of them.
A time or two we actually did that.

Then a deaf girl on the bus
Began to reach out to Eddie.
Literally.

Smiling, she would reach her hand
Across the aisle toward him.

The gesture was not lost on him.
Political correctness, however,
Had not visited Eddie.

Seemingly at random he responded:
At one moment reaching out to touch the hand,
The next moment spitting in her face.

Besides being a dead shot,
His face did not reveal
When he was about to spit.

This deaf girl – the one I can still see
Wiping spit from her face –
What would she do now?

Let's call her Maggie.
Maggie, age 15, had distinguished herself
By a relentless search for a boyfriend.

She told her friend that she talked funny –
Which was an extreme exaggeration –
And was not optimistic of success.

Success – what was that?
What would it look like
When eventually she found it?

Maggie and her friend
Were planning their lives, of course –
And disagreed about the likes of Eddie.

Maggie hoped never to have a baby like Eddie –
Silent, disruptive, unapproachable.

"But you don't know if you're gonna git one,"
Said her friend

"And if you do,
You gotta love him
And take care of him."

The adolescent dialogue raged on.
What to do with the likes of Eddie
Seemed strictly peripheral to it all.

The days passed.
And the children continued to duck.

Then one day I was blindsided.
I was at the wheel at the time,
But it had nothing to do with another vehicle,

'Just another morning on the bus,
Driving along,
Until I looked in the mirror.

There was Maggie, the deaf girl,
Grinning slightly,
Sitting in the seat with Eddie!

Like she belonged there or something.
Playing patty cake.
Holding his hand.

Whatever it took.

Eddie was ecstatic.
Inhibitions were unknown to him,
And soon he was screaming
And jumping up and down.

By the afternoon run
Two others had joined in Maggie's project!

A deaf boy,
First of the three to reach the bus,
Went directly to the seat by Eddie.

He took up where Maggie had left off.

But soon Maggie's girlfriend –
Assigned to the short bus for behavior problems –
Demanded the seat next to Eddie.

All three of them knew exactly what to do –
And Eddie flip-flopped
Between contentment and ecstasy.

KYD, 2007

LISTEN TO YOUR MAMA

A true story.
Time and place: On a special-ed. school bus, 2007
Wide, Weird, Wonderful World Cycle

Tina was a skinny little girl,
With big, thick glasses.

In the wisdom of the school district
She received an individual ride home,
'No other kids on my bus.

We wondered about her:
Why was she on the short bus?

Her balance and coordination were fine.
She could speak and understand speech
 (Without reading lips).
She even had excellent manners.

We got it down to two things:
Either she was legally blind,
Or she had a psych diagnosis.

Tina generally didn't talk about herself.
But one of the other drivers,
In a "How was your holiday" conversation,
Found out that the girl's mother was dead.

We dropped Tina every day
At her father's place —
And she went skipping happily to the door.

She was courteous but direct with us,
Cheerful but not patronizing.

 "You're late," she would say matter-of-factly,
If we were a few minutes later than usual.

And she made it clear —
It was not alright to move the bus,
Not even a foot or two,
 'Til she clicked her seat belt.
Safety rules supported her on this, of course.

"For a compulsive person,"
I thought to myself,
"She's awfully easy to get along with."
And I gave her credit for that.

Rarely did a compulsive kid
Manage their differences from others
As gently as this one did.

Sitting aft,
During the other driver's turn to drive,
I began to watch her.

Sometimes this mysterious little girl
Would respond to conversational pleasantries –
Occasionally even initiate them.

Other times her attention would switch –
Sometimes rather suddenly –
To the direction of the window.

Then she would converse,
Generally for the rest of the ride,
With her unseen companion there.

"Well she's psychic for Heaven's sakes,"
I told myself one day.
It took me much too long
To figure that out.

Her faithful companion showed up every day,
For the brief bus ride.
The girl was happy and skipping afterward,
And obviously was counseled no mischief.

"It's her mother!" I said to myself finally –
And I knew right away that this was true.

So I assured her mother one day –
After the girl got off the bus –
That their conversations were safe here.

I would not interrupt,
Nor call attention to them.

Then one day —
The last day of school it was —
I bought little half-dollar gifts:

For about ten kids on my other route,
And one for Tina, of course.

Which pencil
With a little animal on the end
Would she like?

She made a careful choice,
And was delighted with the gift.

But a few minutes later came the surprise,
As she was getting off the bus:

She gave me a gift,
A well-worn book she was carrying,
"Tricks Animals Play."

This was nothing she came planning to give me —
 Nothing you would get as a gift for the driver —

It was a decision made right there.
And a precious gift it turned out to be.

She gave me a prized possession, it seems –
Something that I'm no good at doing.

And it may be just the shock I've been needing,
To get me out of my packrat ways.

Now I ask you:
How could anyone on Earth
Know the power of that particular gift
At that particular time?

They couldn't.
Her mama made her do it!

        KYD
        1 June 2007
        Tulsa

LENNIE:
Wisdom Without Cleverness

A true story.
Time and place: Seattle, Early nineties
Every Day Heroes Cycle

Lennie worked as a dishwasher.
His counselor helped him handle his money.

His buddy Ted, age 60, rode his bike every day,
Pulling a small wagon that I helped him hitch to it.

One day Lennie came by the office
And said to his counselor,

"Brenda, I want to buy Ted a new bike.
Here's the ad for the model he wants."

"That will take a lot of money out of your account,"
She said responsibly.

Lennie had to talk to
A couple of supervisors that day,
But he persevered.
He had a right to buy that bicycle.

Brenda had a good sense of humor, however,
And afterward she asked him:
"Lennie, could you buy me a bike too?"

"I can give you a hundred dollars toward it,"
He said matter-of-factly.

He didn't get the joke.

                    KYD, 21 January 1998

JERI'S BIG SCORE

A true story.
Time and place: A city on the West coast of the
                  U.S., 1991 and earlier
Every Day Heroes Cycle

Growing up disabled you are protected from things:

Protected from injury.
Protected from disappointment.
Protected from trying things.
Protected from learning.
Protected from growing.

A disabled friend tells me
His people look older than they are
And act younger than they are.

Another disabled person I knew
Was learning to ride the bus.

She didn't know what the walk light
At the corner meant.
And she didn't know what the destination sign
On the bus meant.

She was able to cross the street, and ride the bus;
But she hadn't been allowed to learn.

After 500 in-home assessments
With folks who grew up disabled,
I had learned to expect
The additionally disabling effects
Of all that overprotection.

I was wrong about Jeri, however.

Jeri was disabled since birth.
She grew up using a power wheelchair.
Her hands were just usable enough
To work the controls.

So how did she alone grow up
Not showing signs of
What some of us call the overprotection syndrome?

Without telling you too much private stuff,
Jeri and her sisters spent a lot of time on the streets.

Generally Jeri passed up
Certain recreations and enterprises,
But she was there to see it all
In her mother and in her sisters.

When the welfare worker came,
Jeri was the one conscious enough to do the talking.

When her sisters got in trouble,
Jeri saw how they got out of it

Jeri grew up street smart, agency wise,
And with all the life experience of disability –
Except she was spared the overprotection.

In her twenties, Jeri's friends
From Cerebral Palsy School
Called constantly with their questions
And their problems.
And Jeri talked them through it.

Jeri had a big problem, however,
Which took her longer to solve:
Jeri wanted to work.

Oh, the disability check came every month.
And Jeri knew how to find the services
To make her money stretch.

She had nothing against money, of course.
But the main thing, Jeri told me, was
She wanted to work.

Jeri tried computers.
She found an agency, of course,
That sprang for a computer and lessons.

But Jeri's hands were much too slow.
I think she didn't have the turn of mind for it either.

Finally I had sense enough
To ask her about her vocational choice.

"I really wanted to be a counselor," she said,
"But they told me
You need a master's degree for that."

"Oh Lordy!" I said, forgetting myself.

"Is this about the money or the work?"
"I just want to work," she said.

I told her she would have
No house in the country,
Then we got to work.

She didn't need a salary.
She didn't need an employer.
She didn't need a degree.

We went halves on some cheap business cards.
"Jeri blank, peer advocate," she decided on.
Phone number, too.

She needed reminding
That she already had her clients.
The phone was still ringing.

We did briefings and debriefings at first,
For each client contact.
Later we briefed only occasionally.

Soon came Jeri's big score:

An old friend,
Like many in the disabled community,
Was being held against her will in a foster home.
<u>This</u> situation, however,
Was professionally indefensible.

An abuse complaint had gone nowhere,
When Jeri's friend/client
Was not interviewed in a secure setting.
This time it was different.

Jeri invited her friend to her house
For a couple of days.
(They were not burdened
By professional constraints.)

The first day they saw a protective services worker.
Next day, documentation in hand,
They saw Jeri's client's case manager.

"I'm not going back there," said Jeri's friend.
"She doesn't have to," said Jeri.
They were so right.

The friend got an apartment and an attendant.
And Jeri got a very nice
Para-professional reputation.

>   KYD
>   17 April 2004
>   El Pauji, Venezuela

WHEELCHAIR WARRIOR

A true story.
Time and place: A city on the West coast of the
                  U.S., Mostly 1991
Every Day Heroes Cycle

Karen's parents put her in a foster home.
It's what the doctors said to do.

The foster parents gave her
A very nice room in the back,
All wheelchair accessible,
And took her to church on Sundays.

"Don't leave the house without permission,"
They told her.
"We're responsible for you."

"She has the mind of an eight-year-old,"
They told me when I visited the house.

Karen, at the age of 29, asked to live independently–
Like her friend from Cerebral Palsy School.

No way, they said.
"If you ever leave here
The only place you'll ever go
Is to a nursing home."

Karen hatched a scheme with her friend:

With some convincing, the foster parents
Let her visit her friend
For a couple days.
Quickly the workers were called in:

First day, the protective services worker,
About something the foster parents
May have done
That they didn't learn in church.

Second day, Karen's case manager,
To hear that she was not going back
To that family under investigation.

The scheme worked perfectly!
The worker put Karen in a hotel for a few days,
Then got her an apartment
With a live-in attendant.

Karen was living independently!
With very little preparation,
And a lot of skills to learn.

On a Sunday we went to a bus stop.
She failed in her first attempt to get on a bus,
And missed the chance to go to her church.

"Let's try again next week," we agreed,
As I dropped her at her house.

Away I went, but Karen wasn't through.
She went right back to that bus stop,
And took a ride,
And visited the foster parents!

They were the only family she knew,
And family was important to Karen.

Karen thought her birth family was long gone.
I thought so too.

Now jump forward five months:

Christmas season.
A little holiday visit to Karen's house.

While I'm there her father drops by!
Her real father!

For 29 years, it seems,
The real parents got the news on Karen
From the foster parents.

"She has the mind of an eight-year-old.
We watch her closely.
We won't let her go to a nursing home."

Suddenly the news dried up.
"What do you mean she moved out?!"

They came out of hiding and visited Karen themselves.
It was the only thing they could do.

Karen was very, very happy.
She had her freedom and her parents too.
Her progressive, coastal city
Had been very good to her.

After a year or so,
Her attendant made plans to leave.
He would move to a much different, inland city –

Theocratic in its history,
Very inaccessible to wheelchair folks.
Not friendly either
To the attendant's gender orientation.

His mother lived there however.
He had grown up there.
Now he was going home.

He had begun as a good attendant for Karen,
But now a good friend.

A champion of her escape to freedom.
His importance right up there, I suspect,
With Karen's friend from Cerebral Palsy School.

Karen would go too!
She announced her decision.

Some of us questioned her,
In our professional way:

"Have you thought about
What you're leaving behind?"

"Do you really want to live
Where it's much more difficult than here?"

"That town hasn't even heard of
The invention of curb ramps."

She came back for a visit in a couple of years.
Great suntan.
Same big smile.
Same quick and happy laughter.

Karen's story goes on and on.
I just haven't heard it yet.

But the heart that dares these things,
The heart that inspires these things,
Goes on and on.

KYD
17 April 2004
El Pauji, Venezuela

PREACHING TO A DOG

A true story.
Time and place: Abadiania, Brasil
                  18 June 2008
Crazy Love Cycle

"Excuse me, but
I was really worried
About your safety just now.

"When you ran after that car
It looked like
You were about to be run over.

"You know, you could get a leg run over,
Or your head run over –
And this old body of yours
Might never be the same."

He listened patiently,
So I continued –
One old guy to another.

I petted him, there in the street
By the spiritual hospital.
And told him that I love him very much.

This old dog I have been seeing
For years on that street.

My friend Walter insists
That they chase only
Certain bicyclists and motorcyclists –
And cars too –
Because those are the ones
With the negative energy.

I can't tell
Whether he's right or not.

"I'm sure that you know best
Whether it's really your job
To Chase them.

"But if you would stay
Just a little further back
When you chase them,
You will be a lot safer."

Another car approached just then.

"Try it and see
If it works for you that way!"

He barked his challenge as always –
But stayed to the side!

Only as the car passed
Did he rush it,
Then chased it from behind.

I thanked him kindly
Then continued down the road.

Probably Saint Francis
Would have counseled him much better.

KYD
18 June 2008
Abadiania, Brasil

THE WOMAN WHO SAW TOO MUCH

A true account of what I saw and was told.
Time and place: New Jersey, Probably 1998
Wide, Weird, Wonderful World Cycle

They had you on drugs for <u>something</u>.

So after a day with you at the boardwalk,
And seeing all the gentleness in you,
I figured they got you for seeing too much.

It happens all the time, you know.

I think the majority of the staff
Assigned to your group home
Know in their hearts that you're right.

Whenever I ask them in a friendly way,
They usually cop to it.

So I asked you something
After the others were dropped off:

Like, do you remember before you were born?
Or, do you often see the angels around you?

You spoke freely about it then.
And my great accomplishment for the day
Was to hear you out—

A staff person who did not
Try to stuff your words.

I drove the van toward your group home,
Down quiet country roads.

You sat there in the darkness,
Your voice clear and gentle.

You didn't want to come here.
This lifetime was forced on you, you said.

You continued to disagree with "them" about it,
And hoped to be out of here soon.

So many things I wanted to say to you then!

"Try not to leave too soon
And have to repeat
The same lessons over again."

"What's it like over there?
I've forgotten all of it myself."

"Your house staff seem like decent folks.
You say you can't speak
With any of them about this?"

"Can a soul really be forced to come in?"

But the road to your house was too short.

I saw you only one more time, I think;
The van full of more or less happy travelers,
Heading out for somewhere.

A big, friendly guy,
With no boundaries at all,
Was sitting behind you.

He sang a gospel song for the group.
But then he started touching you.

You had seen his act before,
And were pretty much irate.

So I stopped the van and walked to the side door.
I invited you to change seats.

But you thought I was blaming you
And refused, until I explained:
It was a choice for you,
To get out of his reach.

A month earlier had I not shown you
Some basic respect for who you are?
Or is *any* staff person at *any* time
Likely to treat you insensitively?

I quit that job a few years ago,
And have no chance of seeing you again.
But your memory lingers on:

The clever and sensitive woman
On the boardwalk.
The clear and gentle voice in the night.
Incarcerated in a group home.
Taught that any staff person can slight you.

At one time I would sit and fantasize
About getting you out of there.

I would start a group home,
And invite you, and a few other slighted ones.

I would help you get off your meds,
And you would blossom,
And decide not to die so soon.

Soon the fantasy stopped coming,
And now I just wonder from time to time:
Are you alive or are you dead?

For next time around anyway,
I invite you to a world no longer scared

Of those who see too much.

KYD
1 June 2004
Abadiania, Brasil

NASSAU

A true story.
Time and place: Nassau in the Bahamas
                                Late Nineties
Wide, Weird, Wonderful World Cycle

"Mister, Mister, excuse me,
His feet are dragging on the ground!"

The woman from the tourist trap
Obviously was upset as she ran out of her store.

My friend has very little ability to speak,
So the explanation was left to me:

 "He chooses not to have
Footrests on his wheelchair.
My employer provides travel assistance,
Not equipment."

She was not convinced.
Not at all.

I discussed it with her at length,
While I saw my friend's increasing agitation.

This was a personal freedom issue for him!
He had little enough control over his own affairs,
And this was a choice he had managed to make.

By the time ten different people approached us,
In the space of a few blocks on our tourist stroll,
He seemed to be cursing them out –
'Though no one knew exactly what he was saying.

From 20 years of pushing
People's wheelchairs in the States,
Always a few of them dragging their feet,
I knew what to expect:

Now and then someone would mention it,
Walking by, without stopping.

Nothing prepared me for this.
And when we reached the public market
Where the poor people sell, guess what:

More challenges. A lot more!
The first was a guy who got up in my face.

My friend had me strap him into his chair each day.
Generally this kept him from falling out,
But now it stopped him
As he lunged at the man!

My cousin says the cultural difference I saw
Was about minding our own business.

But I think it's about living by the heart.

                    KYD, In the weeks following the event

THE FUNERAL WITH EVERYTHING

A true story.
Time and place: Casa de Dom Inacio and nearby
                  Abadiania, Brasil
                  6 August 2008
Wide, Weird, Wonderful World Cycle

"You're needed over there.
There's a dog who seems to be dying,"
Said my friend Robert.

My heart leapt
As I rushed around a flower bed
At the Casa de Dom Inacio.

There were mostly three dogs
Who hung around that spiritual hospital;
And I loved them all.

And there she was,
Sweetie Pie,
The female of the three.

Twenty pounds or so.
Skinny.
Mostly white.

She was rather young,
And I had met her
Only that year.

After we introduced ourselves,
She had taken to biting my foot
As I walked down the street –

A helpful reminder
To stop and be sociable.

She helped with chasing the motorcycles too,
On the street in front of the Casa.

Once I had seen her
Knocked head over buns
By one of them.

She had hurried off
Before I could get to her –

But had showed up alive and well
Next day at the Casa,
For her duties as greeter.

Now, weeks later,
She was not to be so fortunate.

I found her *in extremis*,
Poisoned by one of those
Who hate street dogs.

And quickly the poison would kill her!

Carefully I pulled her
To the shade of a tree,
Then waited the hour more
That it took the poison
To do her in.

A hand on her heart,
The other under her head,
I watched with her 'til her moment.

There was much to do in that hour.
A mantra to sing to her.
Children stopping to be counseled.

But mine was a minor role there.

A Buddhist lady, stopping by,
Chanted for the soul
As her moment came —

And so assured her safe arrival home.

The two other Casa dogs came by —
Not needing to be summoned.

The smallest of the three
Guarded his friend,
Before and after her passing.

He was a bit feisty anyway,
But now he barked ferociously
If any of the wrong persons should walk by.

Dogs of the Casa know exactly
Whom they will trust and whom not.

Now this one made gestures
Of rushing at the bad guys.

And later,
As we carried the body up the street
To a beautiful spot for burial,
He joined in —
Lending security to the procession.

Just before the burial orchard
One little boy joined in,
As we passed by his family's tiny home.

At the orchard
He picked immediately the right spot,
Then joined in digging the grave;
And found two perfect pieces of wood
To make a cross.

A minister,
From a new age church in Berkeley,
Prayed beside the grave.

The hostess of the orchard
Served tea and crackers.

And now, I wondered to myself,
Could anyone fill the role,
Left open by Sweetie Pie
When she passed away?

Next morning, walking to the Casa,
It was with an empty feeling that I went.

But as I entered the grounds,
There I saw —

Loving all the guests as they arrived,
Darting about to explore new turf —

A new dog!

Twenty pounds or so.
Skinny.
Mostly white.

But this one
With brown speckles all over —
Resembling now the dirt
With which we had covered the other.

And so I am reminded
Of a saying in the Bible:

 "He will not leave you
Without a comforter."

KYD
9 August 2008
Abadiania, Brasil

PIGEON TALK

A true story.
Time and place: Puntarenas, 2004
Wide, Weird, Wonderful World Cycle

"Cluck cluck cluck," she or he said —
Or noises to that effect.

Walking down a quiet street in Puntarenas,
A very old seaport in Costa Rica,
I turned a corner and there she was.

"Cluck cluck cluck." She walked a small circle,
As I stepped off the curb to avoid her.

She walked 'round and 'round another pigeon
Dead on the sidewalk.

Such a pointed enactment it was
That I stopped to watch,
As she went 'round and 'round.

 Only then did I remember
A peculiar grace transmitted to me
By a mighty teacher many years before.

"You can help transition souls to Heaven,"
He said. "Ground yourself and do such and such.
The spirits have set you up for it."

Now and then,
Passing a graveyard,
I had helped a soul along.

Even a deer carcass on the highway
Might get my attention.

But this tiny, dead pigeon,
On the sidewalk by the park —

He would have received just enough attention
To keep me from stepping on him.

"<u>Cluck</u> <u>cluck</u>," said his faithful friend,
Circling and circling.

"I know you can help!
Now come on!
Do your job!"

I adjusted my energies for the simple task —
And only then did she
Quiet down and step aside.

She moved off a few feet
And waited,
'Til her friend was safely home.

Then, our little service completed,
She strode off –
Joining a couple of others
Across the street.

And I alone remained,
Struggling to comprehend what had just happened.

        KYD
        21 May 2007
        Tulsa

TOO BUSY:
A Lament

A true story.
Time and place: Tulsa, Early November, 2005
Not Classified As To Cycle

He died quietly that Saturday morning
Without complaint,
My partner and me holding him down.

He trusted us even then.

But it took four lethal injections
To stop the heart of that tiny, miracle kitty.

"He has throat cancer, inoperable,"
Said the vet, best one in town

"It would be cruel to let him live 'til Monday,"
Insisted my partner, best cat wrangler in town.

This was my beloved François
Whom I loved like no other –
But never had time to pet or talk with
For more than a minute at a time.

Precious François, never socialized
In proper cat etiquette,
Yet he got along without incident
With all our seven other outdoor cats.

Amazing François, disabled from birth,
Poorly coordinated, unable to vocalize –
He slept serenely in the yard,
Never bothered by stray dogs.

Peacemaker François, right beside me one day,
As we gently counseled another cat
Who had been bullying her sister.

Fed and brushed only by my partner Gemini,
Enlightened Francois, alone of all our kitty clan,
Loved me equally.

Then I, healing student of 20 years duration,
Said okay, put him down.

I had no time to heal him either.

KYD
18 December 2005
Abadiania, Brasil

WHAT'S A WARRIOR TO DO?
A Tribute

A true story.
Time and place: Beginning in East Harlem
                  1970 onward
Crazy Love Cycle

When our hero was just two and a half
His mother took him visiting a lot.
One day he showed them
Who he was going to be.

He went with his mother to see
A friend with a small baby.

Crying in her crib,
The baby was ignored
By both of the mothers
Talking nearby.

"The baby's crying," said the boy —
Two or three times,
With increasing exasperation.

Getting no response from the baby's mother,
He stepped right up
And kicked her in the shin.

What's a warrior to do?

His mother told the story
With great delight.
And so does the author now.

The boy's father also
Treasured that story
Told of his son.

With this and so many other stories
The mother painted the boy a wonder-child,
From whom greatness would be expected.

The boy's father also
Admired the child
As much as anyone –
But soon became uneasy.

"Why must she go on so about him?"
He began to ask himself.

Not for any sensible reason did he worry,
But only because he had
"Been there, done that" –
Or so he thought at least.

Regaled with stories and test scores,
The father's parents and teachers both,
In that small town of his youth,
Had avowed he must do great things –

And so leaned on him
With their demands.

Having spent as much energy then
Fending them off as growing up,
Now he recoiled at the thought:

Would his beautiful and precious son
Bear that same burden too?!!

He had in his own life
Avoided a different pitfall
Which had held his father back.

"A successful life,"
He had said quite often,
"Is one in which some important thing
Turns out better than it had
For the parent of the same sex."

Now he must strike quickly,
And protect his little boy
From the father's own danger —
That of having too much praise.

The same trip, when run on him,
Had been such a curse, he thought,

And reason enough it seemed for
All those underachieving years.

That wasn't much of a reason,
He'll tell you now.
Denial is denial, after all.

But being a young father,
Full of such conviction,
Never would he let his own son
Suffer from the very same thing!

However the boy's mother,
As anyone with a divorce will know,
Would take no direction from that man.

Her good buddies in the 'hood,
If she should leave the boy at home,
Would gather 'round to ask
"Where's the old man today?"

Wise and confident beyond his years,
Their son had a following already
Before he was three.

So what could be wrong with that?

Raised a racial minority
In this country where they were,

Her buddies knew all about getting
Too little respect —

But had little means
In their experience, to conceive
Of suffering from too much.

So how was the father alone to stop it then?
There's the rub.

A classic dilemma it seems he had,
Brought round and round
In the lives of single parents everywhere.

And likely he was not even the first
To try the tragic solution
Which soon would come to mind:

"Nothing to it but to offset it!"

If the mother would praise in excess,
He would praise his son hardly at all.

Similarly, volatile as the mother was,
The dad must be even more taciturn
Than he by nature was.

And when he drank and did his drugs –
Which was pretty much every day,
All the years that the boy was growing up –

He would see himself so superior,
Since all he did was ignore the boy
So he could run with the women.

Now how do you think
This was gonna turn out?

Growing with the years then,
As a young teenager
The son would watch his mother's back
As she staggered from the bar at night.

The father had no offset for this —
Unless to try that old tactic,
And not to compliment him much
For all that courage shown.

"Let him alone!"
He told himself.

A virtue that arose
Without ever being taught
Would need no daddy elbowing in
To take the credit for it.

It created itself,
So let it nurture itself too.

Even that father knows,
These thirty years later,
What awful and destructive nonsense
He had told himself.

And appealing that nonsense was
For that father who had lost,
Somewhere along the way,
So much of his ability to feel.

<u>Still the Warrior stood.</u>

There was not all the sweetness
Of his toddler years –
But the father seemed not to reflect
On that so much.

When the son was seventeen,
His dad would not sign for him
To enter early the Marines –

And in fact convinced the mother
Not to sign either.

The day before the son went in,
At the age of eighteen,
That father had his last drink.

Sobering it was the next day,
To wake and find
The son had drunk it all.

"He will have a hard time
With John Barleycorn," he thought,
"And I must get sober to help."

Fat chance!
The father stayed sober all right,
But found no way to help.

"My mother raised me to be a criminal,"
The son would tell his grandmother
Many years later,
"And my father didn't raise me at all."

Even hearing of the son's report
Was not enough for the father.

Too little too late it was,
For that father to avoid
The tragedy soon to come.

A year or two later
Came the confrontation.

Sitting in that very grandmother's yard,
Angrily the son, now nearly forty,
Recalled for his father the painful times
In their years together.

While this unconscious father,
Lacking in the feelings that befit his role,
Did not know to just shut up and cry.

This unknowing father,
Confused by his own risks and sacrifices
Which seemingly had done no good,
Now tried what he thought was
Reasoning with his son:

This was not so good –
But what about that?

The father knew not how to cry –
And the son had not come to negotiate.

And so that son
Did like many a
Neglected son before him:

He demanded an amends
Impossible for the father,
As it would forsake another.

An amends that would put an end also
To how the father would live
The rest of his own life.

And so it was the son,
Hurtfully ignored all those many years,
Was in effect ignored again.

Very well then –
He would not speak
To his father any more
Unless his demand were met.

So in the years since then,
As any parent might well imagine,
That father has learned to cry very well.

And very easy was it to learn,
Aided by the natural consequences
Of his own behavior.

And the son, telling folks now
That he <u>has</u> no father
Continues to suffer from that father's coldness
Which for him still exists.

KYD, 1 July 2008
Casa de Dom Inacio
Abadiania, Brasil
Revised April 2010
Revised July 2010

'Never missed a beat

'NEVER MISSED A BEAT

A true story.
Time and place: Stewartsville
                  13 April 2009
Every Day Heroes Cycle

"I'm ready to go," she said.
"I've been waiting for God
To call me home.

"Many years ago
I gave my life to Jesus.
I know that I'm going to Heaven."

Yeah, Yeah, Yeah.
For several years she'd said she was ready.

Clearly she was convinced of it –
But what depth could it have?

Sold since childhood she was, on one of
Many mutually exclusive religions:

Each telling in their kinder moments
What a shame it was –
That the others could not
Join them when they go to Heaven.

I'd been there, done that:
Raised in my mother's Protestant Christianity.

Later I kicked out the anthropomorphic God –
Who answered to only one name,
Who offed folks who followed others,
Who granted only one lifetime to get it right.

"Have no other gods before me" indeed!
The God of my heart these days
Doesn't even care about my philosophy.

Oh, He/She looks forward, certainly,
To the day when I will get over
Whatever I happen to believe this year.

He/She cares for the intellect
In the same inscrutable ways
That She/He cares for
Whatever else I'm made of.

But to get bent out of shape
When a person doesn't subscribe to
A particular one of those
Narrow little systems?

Gimme a break!

Stories known to me are of
Folks who head out for Heaven
Believing that stuff – and have
A lot to adjust to Over There.

"Now hold on, it's a little worse that that."
I must have reasoned somehow.

If it were just the shock
Of finding an exotic Heaven,
She could handle it.
She'd have to!

I might then have expected
To see her cruise right out of here
As her time came –

Buoyed by a headful of superstitions –
Counseling relatives in their grief –
All that sort of story!

Only I didn't expect that.

The veil, known even
To some of the narrower Christians,
Seems to have a few tricks to it!

Held responsible for
The Heavenly "needs to know" screening,
The veil could only be a lot slicker than
Us guys it's hiding stuff from! Right?

It's only being nice,
I'm sure of that.
No nasty tricks to get us in trouble
Or catch us up short!

It's about keeping out distractions –
Letting folks concentrate
On what's up while we're here.

However, following my train of thought,
Senility, and other transitional episodes
Near the end of life, are seen as
A chance to peek ahead,
To begin to see what's over there.

But exceeding the bounds even
Of senile revelation
Is another knowingness:

At our high and dramatic moments
We act as if
We know more than we do:
So what will we use to explain that?

The subconscious, you may call it.

And that's what I feared all along
Would trip her up,
When the end of her life came into view.

Her fundamentalist philosophy
Would be so confounded by intimations
Of the actual greatness of a God —

That her demeanor at least
Would show a crack or two.

Not fear, because
There's nothing to be afraid of;
But some sort of wonder,
Confusion even.

And so I managed, never mind the awkwardness
Seen everywhere in my existence,
To be there when
Finally the bumbling doctor said
"Yes, you have cancer in the lung."

If ever there was a moment
For a son to watch closely —
For a poet to watch closer yet —
This was it.

Hey, she never missed a beat:

I drove her home,
And she sat right down
To list whom she would tell;

And whom she would not.

Good, practical reasons she had
For those choices too, and for
Which treatments to accept or refuse.

Straightaway she called
A niece and a nephew,
With her matter-of-fact report –

Telling afterward that
The niece had expected it –
And worrying for the first time
In all of this,
Because the news had hit the nephew hard.

Then she went into questions like,
To whom to give yesterday's Easter candy
That she didn't like

'Never missed a beat.

That night she did sleep
Twice as long as usual –
And seemed none the worse for it
In the morning.

God, it seems, really doesn't care
About my mother's philosophy either.

More than that, God
May not need to correct her on it
'Til she gets over there.

> KYD
> 14 April 2009
> (Before my mother's death)
> Stewartsville

PHILOSOPHY AND DOUGHNUTS

A true story.
Time and place: Warren County, New Jersey
                  Forties and thirties
Every Day Heroes Cycle

Somebody ought to put the two of you in a bag
And shake you up," she said.
That was Grandma's take on my complaint.

Generally she didn't do snappy one-liners,
But this was an exception.

I at one extreme on some very minor issue
Now lost in the fog of time.

My long-forgotten adversary —
Not even present at that moment —
Evidently at the other extreme.

To my four-year-oldness
My grandmother's philosophy
Seemed less than helpful at the time.

Many years later however,
I quoted her at my father's funeral:

"They should put us in a bag
And shake us up" —

Those of us over here
Mourning as he leaves,

And those who love him over there
Gathering 'round in joy.

That got a laugh at a funeral
For bleep sake!

And Grandma got a laugh out of me too;
One of those slow laughs –
Several years in coming.

Her metaphor is
From doughnut-making of course.
It's how you get the sugar onto the doughnuts.
I knew that!

We were staying at her house right then.
And Grandma never strayed
Very far from the kitchen.

Her philosophy didn't stray far from there either.
And I believe that served her well.

Take another incident for example,
A few years earlier:

"His father isn't white!"
Says a local guardian of the racial purity
Which never existed anyway.

He had rushed to see my future grandmother
With news of a sighting of my father's father.

"That boy's father sure ain't no white man."
Surely she wouldn't want
Her daughter going out with him.

"He's such a nice boy –
What do I care about this story of yours?"

That's what she told him!
Good old Grandma.

This all took place, mind you,
In a county where
The Klan rode in parades
Ten years before.

When philosophy finds metaphor in the kitchen,
Then we can believe our own eyes.
We don't have to depend
On what the cookbook says.

KYD
Memorial Day 2007
Walker Hall, Tulsa

FAMILY NUT

A sincere account, well-intended, from a person in no
position to be objective.
Time and place: New York, New Jersey,
                   Berkeley, elsewhere
                   1965 through 1998 when written
Wide, Weird, Wonderful World Cycle

Does your family have a designated nut?
Mine does.

I brought her around, actually.
She's my ex-wife.

Now don't think I'm putting her down,
Because I'm not!
Actually I'm very grateful to her, and here's why:

In my country, most families choose
An official nut.
My mother says it wasn't that way in her day.
But times are more challenging now.

Who are we to blame it on?
Bleep happens.

Seems like we've only had that slogan
For a short while,
But it caught on big time.

When bleep happens, who's to take the rap?
Just little stuff.
No cops to come around.
No newspaper stories.
But it takes us out of our program.

Biblically, once a year
The tribe would designate a goat;
An actual four-legged goat,
Ritually made responsible
For all the problems of the past year.

Then they drove that goat out of the village
And that was it!
Quick and neat,
And you never had to talk to that goat again.

But rituals with animals are such a primitive thing!
Aren't they?

Now and then a cult gets busted
For messing with animals,
And you see it on the news.

Most families would never take their problems
To an animal these days,
But still the bleep happens.
It just doesn't quit.
Sometimes it seems like it's actually building up.

"Scapegoat: a person or thing
Bearing the blame for others."
It says that in the dictionary.

These days we use a person.
It's so much more civilized.

So how do you get to be one of these modern,
Politically correct scapegoats?
I've thought about it,
And it's not based on merit so much.
'Bottom line is, it's based on need.

Does someone talk a little too loud?
Do they have a taste for unfashionable causes?
Even a twitch, perhaps.

He buys funky Christmas presents.
She sent that humorous card
To Aunt Mildred and offended her.

Lots of things go wrong in a modern family.
And we're nothing if not quick
In seeking for the cause.

It's more comfortable for the majority, however,
If one person is designated
To be blamed automatically, whenever needed.

And it's all relative, who gets picked.
When the need arises, who fits the profile best?
It doesn't need to be much of a nut
'Though they certainly could be.

When I was a child my uncle nominated me.
But he died early, not living to see me installed.

And the need must not have been so great
In those days,
Because I passed relatively unnoticed
For many years after that.

Later, when our need for a goat
Was much greater,
There was Norma!

And well qualified she was.
Why, she had a note from her doctor,
Calling her a nut.

Confidentiality within families does not exist,
And so, when she was needed,
Her qualifications were well known

We all selected her,
And reelected her at intervals.
There's the evil part!

"Don't give her my new phone number."

"Don't encourage her to go to Seattle;
Relatives there won't want to see her."

"Let me see if he wants to talk to you
On the phone just now, Norma."

A special population of one,
Faithfully taking the blame,
And receiving patronage for doing so.

Norma would not go away.
Neither humiliation nor special treatment
Was too much for her.

We have a son.
And we passed him back and forth
'Til he was grown.

For her there was no question,
But to stay in contact.
The designated family nut provides a service,
Ostensibly a needed one.

Is this perverse?
Certainly.

Is it a sacred piece of the mosaic, all the same?
I think so.

When a nut is needed, one will appear.
If entering the scene as a nut
Is the cost of getting on stage at all,
Then some brave, foolhardy soul
Will answer the heavenly casting call.

There's the divine, crazy part.

So if I thank you Norma
For answering that casting call
It's certainly not sarcastic.
But it may not be from a very high ground
That I speak, either.

It's simple self-interest, I believe.
If not for you, Norma, I would be the one.

KYD
19 February 1998
Stewartsville

GEMINI

A true story.
Time and place: New Jersey
                  Late Nineties
Every Day Heroes Cycle

"Geminiiii," he said,
His voice friendly and playful –
And totally disbelieving.

She already knew
That inflection in his voice.

She was "staff" –
But not the kind that puts you down
Or orders you around.

Her job was
To drive him around on Tuesdays –
So that's what she did:

To the store,
To appointments;

'Even hearing his stories
Now and then.

Nearly always he had been comfortable
With her gentle but active listening.

Now it was his turn.

He knew what they put you on meds for.
He saw it all around him.
Gemini fit that picture.

So now he had asked her,
"What meds are you on, Gemini?"

"None," she said.

"Geminiiii!"

He *seemed* to know her pretty well –
All these months of driving him around,
Nothing but honesty and being herself.

Just the plain truth . . .
But there's the rub

Her caricature of a professional manner
Met the muster where she worked –
Most of the time anyway.

But there was nothing in her
That wanted to talk about her courage,
Or her passion for the work.

These were not topics.
Not for her conversations with others –
Not even with herself.

She chose consciousness over comfort.
Over a popular image.
Over an easy passage in the world.
That's why she used no meds.

She needed that consciousness
As she cared for others.
It hurt sometimes.
But it's what she had that worked.

Geminiiii!!

KYD
25 March 2008
Tulsa

Gemini

JUST RIGHT

A true story – but I can't prove it.
Time and place: A few years ago
Wide, Weird, Wonderful World Cycle

There was a man
So clumsy in his spiritual life
That he couldn't even sit still to meditate.

Detachment was some ten letter word.
Didn't people ever
Fight their way into Heaven?
He had heard of that somewhere.

Actually, he had never planned
To live a spiritual life at all.
It just grew on him somehow.

Now he set out on a spiritual path
All his own –
But only because
There seemed nothing else to do.

His broken down heart –
Which he had despised and neglected
In a lifetime long ago –
Now served not at all to inform him
As he blundered along.

He found a woman to love him, however –
And even a spiritual teacher
To put up with him as well.

Carefully the teacher watched him –
Getting himself in and out of
Some ridiculous situation,
Learning a bit from it –
Then blundering again.

To his own eyes,
Only his enthusiasm
Seemed to sustain him at all.

Then one day,
As one thing or another
Came out in their conversations,
The teacher picked up on something:

"Your partner is holding you back,"
She told him.

"Do you realize that
She doesn't even believe
In the path that you're on?"

Yes, he already knew.
But he didn't tell the teacher that.

His partner's spiritual path
Was so different from his own,
That they could hardly even talk about it.

"You have a future life contract,"
The teacher had said, "for
Some very great cosmic responsibility."

"But what about my partner's great love for me?"
He said to himself, driving home.
"Already that has made me a better person."

He looked now at his life-long history –
As a man unreliable and unresponsive
In love relationships.

And he thought of his teacher's warnings:
Not to waste time, on the way
To his great spiritual destiny!

A couple more times it came up,
Talking with his teacher –
And still he said nothing.

Then one day she found it out:
"You're letting her hold you back!"
Her voice rang with amazement.

The fairies on the windowsill –
Witness to the whole series of conversations –
Fluttered with excitement!

"What will he say to this one?"

"In my creation," he said,
Shrugging his heart,
"We will have enough time
To do things just right."

The man stayed with his partner.
But it was only after a few years
That he realized:

"We already have enough time
To do things right.
We have exactly enough time
To do things perfectly right."

KYD,
3 August 2007
Abadiania, Brasil

<h1 style="text-align:center">XENOMORPH</h1>

A true story.
Time and place: Tulsa, 2005
Wide, Weird, Wonderful World Cycle

I saw you in that parking lot:

Your overpriced car blocking traffic.
Stuck, halfway into a space,
'Couldn't go forward or back.

"If you had to do anything practical for a living
You'd probably starve. Wouldn't you?!"

That was the cab driver
Bus driver
Delivery driver in me:
Grumbling silently at you,
Waiting out a ten second traffic jam.

A minute later
Gym bag in hand,
I walked up that same lane.

There was that same shiny car,
Same dumb predicament.

But it wasn't you anymore!
You were not your car.

Now you stood beside it.
Small, thin woman.
Dark hair.
Oriental accent.

For a moment I tried to avoid your eyes.
Then it all melted.

"Can you help me?
Get car into parking space?"

Of course I parked your car for you.
It's a whole lot different
When you're a person, not a car.

'Many years of professional driving,
Many years of social service work . . .

Two different habits.
Two attitudes.
Unrelated until today.

Thanks for the lesson.

                    KYD
                    29 May 2005
                    Walker Hall, Tulsa

BURIED ALOFT

A true story.
Time and place: 30,000 feet up
                  With no place to go
Self-Disclosure Cycle

Faithless to an old lover
In a lifetime long ago,

Yeshe reached his second childhood
With a few buttons to go off!

For years he took longer and longer vacations
At a facility for spiritual healing
Of a loving and caring sort.

Making up, one might suppose,
For abandoning that lover long ago
To some inquisitors or such,

Those women he saw now
In greatest distress
Received his tireless attention.

They needed only to ask.

But how had that earlier woman died?
And where in this was the link?

Thinking little about it,
He ran himself to the ground
At his beloved spiritual hospital,
Til the day his flight was to leave –

Then fell exhausted into a seat
On an overnight flight home.

Only when he awoke
An hour or two into the flight

Did he notice the immobilizing device
Which he had accepted for a seat.

Worthy of those same inquisitors
In the devilishness of their craft

That seat now allowed no
Major body part to straighten

"Tantamount to torture,"
Said the International Red Cross
Just a few years before –

Referring then to forced positions,
But evoked now in Yeshe's thought
By the seat he was assigned.

"An inquisitor's an inquisitor,"
He realized a bit later —
And safely away from that plane.

"There's the ones I abandoned her to,
And the ones who got me into that plane."

Karma: The law of return.
Cause and effect.
Equal and opposite reaction.

They got him and now he's free.
No more buttons to push
When a helpless one is seen.

Now he can run and push wheelchairs,
Hold the panicked ones by the hand,

Just for the joy of it
With no more accounts to be settled.

Freedom comes in many ways
And most of them are welcomed.

KYD
3 March 2011
Tulsa

ELLIE'S MANTRA

A true story.
Time and place: Tulsa, Oklahoma
                  Approximately 2003
Every Day Heroes Cycle

"There's a teaching," said Sister Ellie,
"Concerning the mantra
'Om mani padme hum.'"

"I don't know whether this is true or not,
But they say if an animal hears that mantra
Then he or she can be a human
In the next lifetime."

Ah, but Ellie was the chaplain
At the local humane society.
They gave her a key to the shelter!

"I'm not sure it's true," she said,
"But when I'm at the shelter,
And there's nobody else around,
I say that mantra to the animals —

"Just in case it's true."

                  KYD
                  1 July 2007
                  Casa de Dom Inacio, Brasil

142

LYING FOR LOVE

A true story.
Time: Around 1999
Every Day Heroes Cycle

Jim couldn't tell the truth two times in a row,
But I trusted him entirely.

His work was serving others.
He even started his own company
In order to serve more freely.

Lying was how he kept that company afloat,
Out there in the business world.

We could feel Jim's joy
As he took people with disabilities
On vacations and outings.

So much joy, in fact,
That he forgot to do the math.

Jim's trips ran at a loss most of the time, I think,
Because he didn't figure out the cost beforehand.

Lying kept him afloat for quite a while,
When the money wasn't there.

He smiled.

And he shared the joy of our guests.
I asked him about his lying,
And told him it wasted a lot of my energy.

Jim worked at telling the truth,
And reminded me joyfully when he did so.

Then his company went bankrupt.

> KYD
> 24 December 2006
> Stewartsville

INSIGHT UNREQUITED

A true story.
Time and place: San Francisco
                  1972 or '73
Wide, Weird, Wonderful World Cycle

"You can't be a Scorpio,
That's impossible!
There must be a mistake about your birth date."

How stunned I was when you told me that!
You were right, of course.
But no way was I going to tell you so.

That's life in hiding, you see.
To have my son with me for a bit
We were hiding from his mother.

And as the price of that
We gave up our identities.
New names. New birth dates even.

You were the first astrologer
Who had ever blown my mind,
So I hadn't known anyone would
See through the phony birth date.

Two things I learned from you
That San Francisco afternoon,
Thirty years ago,
Bicycle messenger to bicycle messenger:

One was that astrology works.
And a year later I was studying it myself.
The other was that secrecy costs us.
And it keeps on costing us.

In fairness, you needed to hear
That yes, I'm no Scorpio.
I confused and misinformed
A sincere and gifted astrologer, that day.

Insight unrequited!

KYD
10 January 2005
Stewartsville, New Jersey

FINE LINE

A true story.
Time: 2003
Wide, Weird, Wonderful World Cycle

Joan hated to ride the buses
Because all the drivers came on to her.

All the male staff where she lived
Showed an inappropriate interest.

And the guys in the house
All made remarks
When she walked down the hall.

Women in the house were jealous,
And didn't set her a place at the table.

That's what Joan said.

Soon a newcomer to the house
Said I had lost her medications.

The woman was beside herself,
Rushing about in a frenzy.

Back and forth in the back yard,
The fastest pacing I'd ever seen.

And right beside her,
Stride for stride,
Arm across her shoulders
There went – you guessed it – Joan.

Soon the woman calmed down.

"I used to work in a nursing home," Joan said,
"And when they got upset,
I was the only one who could calm them down."

I firmly believe
Half of what she says.

KYD, 9 June 2003

PULLING A BELINDA

A true story.
Time and place: Abadiania, Brasil
                  6 and 7 August 2008
Every Day Heroes Cycle

"But you have to have your soup,"
She said with simple conviction.

Both of us had had psychic surgery
The day before.

Both were advised to rest
All the next day –
For the greatest benefit,
And for personal safety.

To make it really clear,
Folks are banned the next day
From the spiritual hospital grounds.

Belinda, a volunteer there,
Had offered to find someone
To bring my healing soup of the day
To the apartment where I stayed.

And so I waited,
Resting as directed –
The body and soul
Soaking up all that nice healing.

Finally a knock on my door;
And who should appear as messenger
But Belinda herself!

I challenged her
In a friendly way,
For not resting at her home
As I was at mine.

But apparently, in her logic,
It was okay to detract from her healing,
If that's what it took
To add to someone else's.

While I lay in bed
Seeing to my recovery,
She, in that same stage of recovery,
Carried soup around the neighborhood,
Seeing to the recovery of others.

Now if I could understand
The laws of spirit,
Even in the simplest way,
Then maybe I could know if she
Might actually heal more perfectly.

She gave away her own healing,
But it wouldn't go!
Some things you just can't give away.

KYD
9 August 2008
Abadiania, Brasil

Alice

ALICE

A true story.
Time and place: Tulsa
                  Probably 2002 and 2003
Crazy Love Cycle

Alice lived outdoors by the river
Until she got her meds straightened out.

Along the way
Her husband left her.

Later, in an emotional processing group,
A housemate of Alice was role-playing a problem
With a stand-in for that woman's current lover.

The stand-in was called out of the room,
Alice stepped in,
And she played him perfectly.

She knew his act
Because the guy was her husband.

KYD, 9 June 2003

Mr. Branco

MR. BRANCO

This is a true story.
Time and place: Abadiania, Brasil
                        A December evening, 2010
Wide, Weird, Wonderful World cycle

The horse's name was Branco,
But all the tourists called him Mr. Ed.

They'd call you that too
If you were an old white horse,

Seen each day on a different block
Trimming slowly the people's lawns.

He never bothered anyone,
And seemed to work part-time
At pulling a man's cart.

Now here's the other hero of our tale,
A guest come for a healing
To that magical mystical place nearby —

A great spiritual hospital
In Branco's Brasillian hometown:

Fred, let's call him, was told
After psychic surgery there

That the spirit entities of the place,
Benefactors to us all,

Demanded one thing from him only
In the day and night which followed:

"Sleep for 24 hours!"
The volunteer had said.

And if you can't sleep
A least lie still —

With your eyes closed,
Alone in your room,

No TV, Heaven forbid,
No phone calls, no guests.

Now dear Fred was a decent chap
Respectful of others he met.

So passing the day and evening then
He did just as he'd been told...

Then came that long night
With no sleep promising to come.

Well maybe just to step out on the lawn –
And for a few minutes alone
He could love up that beautiful sky.

Now what spirit entity,
Fred would like to know,

Could begrudge him those few minutes
To adore the works of God?

No sooner tempted than done then,
Into that peaceful Abadiania night
With not a soul around.

Ah, but what was that noise then
Just behind him where he stood?

Not a footstep exactly, nor the voice
Of any human or a beast

And in his idle curiosity then
Fred just glanced around –

Oh God, Oh no
He'd really done it now!

And a silent apparition
In the form of a white horse

EVERY DAY HEROES

Was there to stare
And catch him at his lapse —

While Fred, brave as the average tourist
Just the moment before,
Now ran back to his bed
Promising never to stray again.

So it's of my readers that I must ask,
As the poet assigned to this tale,

Whether such a horse
On such a night
Could invent this prank alone —

Or whether those spirits,
The very same ones
Who conspire with poets by day,

Might whisper as well
In a horse's ear
In an idiom that suits,

Of a tourist strayed abroad,

Who's left now to ponder
For a very long time —

On that horse
And that night
And those spirits

And on what they will
Think of next!

KYD
29 Dec 2010
Abadiania, Brasil

MARVELOUS MARIO

This is a true story, interpreted any way I want to.
Time and place: At and near Casa de Dom Inacio
                  Abadiania, Brasil
                  Oct. and Nov. 2010
Wide, Weird, Wonderful World cycle

Black Mary
They called him at first –

Noticing only later, that
They'd better say Black Mario.

Now how did this little dog,
I really have to ask,

Relate to them in such a way
That they never turned him over to look?

Then there was the time
By the healing waterfall:

Several of us hiked down
To that holy place,
And stayed between the ropes.

 (The rules are quite specific
About who and where and when.)

And while our buddy Mario
Reminded us what a thrill it was,

The delicious scents and sounds
Of this lush tropical forest,

We humans stayed
Between those ropes.

But Mario, a stray who wandered up
To adopt my friends a month before;

Dear Mario, alert
And quick and curious
As any dog I've seen;

Marvelous Mario,
Never instructed by us
On how that he should act;

Senses alert,
Picking up on all that he could...

Mario stayed between the ropes too!

It's the thing to do, you know.
All the humans were doing it.

Now this was a holy place, remember;
And even I somehow was affected –

Just enough it seems
To remember a passing remark
In one of those books I read:

Are an animal's markings symmetrical –
One side matching the other
In the pattern of its coloring?

Fascinated, I'd been watching
Ever since I'd heard of this –

And here was Mario,
One of very few I'd seen
With nearly perfect markings
By that simple little test.

Well what's it all mean?
Am I gonna tell you or what?

A soul, according to that book –
Its author and title
Long since drifted from my mind –

A soul, when such a marking
Is awarded for this life,

Can only be one
Who in another time
Was a human just like us!

KYD
6 Nov 2010
Abadiania

Martín

YOU CAN'T FOOL A STREET DOG

A true story.
Time and place: Abadiania
                  10 Oct. 2010
Every Day Heroes Cycle

"Now I will get into your book"
He said, laughing nervously
As we parted at my street.

A short block earlier on,
In our walk through
This small South American town,

Is where he showed himself
To be the hero that he is.

Here's how the spirit entities,
Found in this town,
Set him up to stop a fight —
And me to write about it.

Wandering about
On a Sunday afternoon,

First I was drawn
To explore a certain cow pasture —

One I walked by
Many times before
With no curiosity at all.

Then twice I stopped
Because of the heat.

At the second of those stops,
As I blathered to the angels,

Along came Martín!

Now here was a man —
A young guy from Argentina,
Whom all the street dogs
Loved at first sight.

Soon I did too, of course.
You can't fool a street dog.

I sat right then
In front of a spiritual center
Where he led some of our songs —

Ballads simple and beautiful
From the towns of his youth,

Songs that a cultured person
Like himself could love,
Only because his heart
Knew whereof they spoke.

If only you could see him
With a human or a dog,

Then you would know that
Whoever found themself with him
At the scene of a street fight
Was the safest one on the block.

And so it was.

The first thing that happened,
To stop us from our stroll,

Was a man yelling curses
As he threw one motor scooter
On top of another.

Then the other guy –
The owner no doubt –
Chasing him with
A big piece of lumber.

Back and forth
And soon the owner,
If so he was,

Took shelter in a walled driveway
Open at the front;

While the other,
Thrower of the bike,
Now found large stones –

And threw them one after another
Where the foe just now had fled.

Carefully I watched –
Close enough to see a bit,

But far enough away
Not to get involved –

When suddenly I heard a great yell,
And there went Martín
Fast as a person could run;

Charging in to stop two men,
Strangers to him moments before,

From a fight I had blithely assumed
May be exactly what
They both deserved.

Shocked by Martín as he charged
In his absolute abandon,

That thrower of the stones
Backed off just far enough,
Before he realized
He was now out of range.

Then grumbling and cursing –
Looking threatening as he could –

He walked back to the corner,
With Martín just behind,

Now telling him in gentler voice
To go up to the church
And tell the rest of it.

And all I thought
We were going to do

Was watch a small town fight
With a broken head or two.

KYD
10 Oct. 2010
Abadiania

ALEXANDER OF ABADIANIA: THE FATHER'S TALE
A man's great devotion.

A true story.
Time and place: Abadiania, Brasil
                  2003 to 2008
Crazy Love Cycle

I first met Ed
At the Casa de Dom Inacio,
In Brasil.

I should say that I first saw him there.
I was pretty much speechless
For the first couple summers
Of watching him in action,
And I struck up no conversations.

Now I had worked most of my adult life
In the disabilities field,
And thought maybe I had seen it all.

Ed's son had a progressive disease,
And already was in a wheelchair
By the time I first saw them.

So Ed, a young and clever man
With a good career going,
Quit it all
And brought the boy there
For a healing.

Not everyone there
Gets their body healed, however.

The spiritual growth is the thing
That must come first somehow;
And the activities that get you to that
Are different for each person.

So every day for five years
Ed wheeled the boy
To all the healing sessions.

He took him to the cafes to socialize.

They did flexibility and strength routines,
And Ed looked as good
As the therapists I've seen.

I never saw either of them
Looking discouraged or angry.

The boy, with all these adults around,
Was wise and articulate
Beyond his years;
Never flattering or insincere.

And Ed, philosophical and funny by turns,
Appeared to be doing
Only what came naturally for him.

After five years of this –
The boy getting weaker,
His arms like broomsticks –
The pneumonia took him.

Ed was quite a student of his son's disease,
And could have figured out
That the physical miracles
Were not coming.

But when we work that long
And that hard for a miracle,
Of course one comes!

And so the boy goes off to Heaven now,
Spiritual miracles in hand –

There to watch from above,
Strong and confident in his advocacy
For the father who loved him so well.

When they are together again,
There is no limit
To what they will be able to do!

KYD
18 August 2008
Casa de Dom Inacio, Brasil

HOW DO YOU TALK TO AN ANGEL?

A true story.
Time and place: Abadiania
                  Third week of July 2008
Goofy Poets Cycle

"All my life people have taken
A strong liking to me," she said.

It took hours of conversation
To get that and a few other
Bits of evidence out of her.

And by that time she was concerned,
Because I was keeping her from her work.

In a neighborhood adjoining
A healing center in South America,
She pedaled her bicycle every day:

Showing up to push people
In their wheelchairs.

Listening to people
Who asked her to.

Giving away fruit
From her back yard.

Maturing had been unpleasant, she said,
When guys started taking an interest in her.

I wondered about the many times
That she cried so intensely.

She said she was clearing herself
Of some pain.

Only later did I learn that it was
For the suffering in the world that she cried.

She had no clairvoyant abilities, she said,
But had always understood
Certain things in her surroundings.

The causes of violence
And the causes of peace
Were obvious to her from birth.

For a few precious days
Our apartments shared
A common back yard.

And in that time,
If I were wise in any way,
And not just a wandering minstrel,

I might have learned
To turn my whole life around.

Nothing like that happened, however.

To my knowledge, in a long lifetime,
I had known only one other angel incarnate.

I was much younger then,
And from the experience I came away
The author of a love letter.

I did only slightly better this time.
But I'll tell you what doesn't work
For talking with an angel.
Let me count the ways!

Understand now
That these signs
Of who she was
Were shown to me only gradually.

Early on in my blundering
I didn't know who she was.

So don't judge me the fool
That I actually am.

I met her at a talent show,
Where she sang beautiful ballads
In a wee, small voice.

A few days later she happened
To move into that apartment next to mine.

Another of spirit's little coincidences
That we are allowed to see through.

Well, the first thing to report
To you, dear forgiving readers,
Is that I made a pass at her.

Yes I did.

She was obviously unnerved by this,
And retreated to her apartment
Ten minutes later.

Now that ten minutes was for me!
Can you see that?
A mere human
Would have shown my ego
No such mercy.

Well, mornings I like to talk
With the spirit entities,
When I first wake up.

So between thoughts in my sleep,
And a good talking to the next morning,
Even I began to suspect
There was something different
In that next apartment.

And so it was, after my apology,
I began swearing to her
That her self-doubts were groundless.

She had wondered aloud, about
Being in her thirties and
Having no career or profession.
Not a marriage either.

Now I argued that
The sweet and loving acts
That kept her busy all day
Are a career.

Good pay will attract
Plenty of doctors and lawyers.

But she is busy all day
With the plainest and simplest
Of pure, loving acts.

They don't have schools for that.
And they don't have salaries for that.

Lifetimes hence they will,
So I argued.

Days later she was to tell me,
More gently than anyone could,
That all that talk
Had been keeping her from her activities.

She doesn't even call it work.

And so, another night to sleep.
Another waking up conversation,
With those spirits
Who never give up on me.

Boy was I ready for her that next day!

I had figured out that she was angelic,
And now I gave myself one day
To convince her of it.

Well, there's no sarcasm here,
Oddly enough.

I'm sure she is angelic,
I made my case well,
And she's about 50 percent convinced.

It does explain so many things.

But she says it's not that important!!
It's feelings that we need to cultivate,
Not ideas.

Next day I came prepared.

My list of questions was about
How I could help
In her heavenly work.

Since in a couple more days
She would be continents away,

I was determined to find
Something I could do
From a distance.

But I was too late.

For two or three days
She had comforted me,
By listening to all of this.

Now she must be off,
To all her other work!

And what I have learned from this
Is to cry a little better.

KYD, 21 July 2008
Casa de Dom Inacio, Brasil

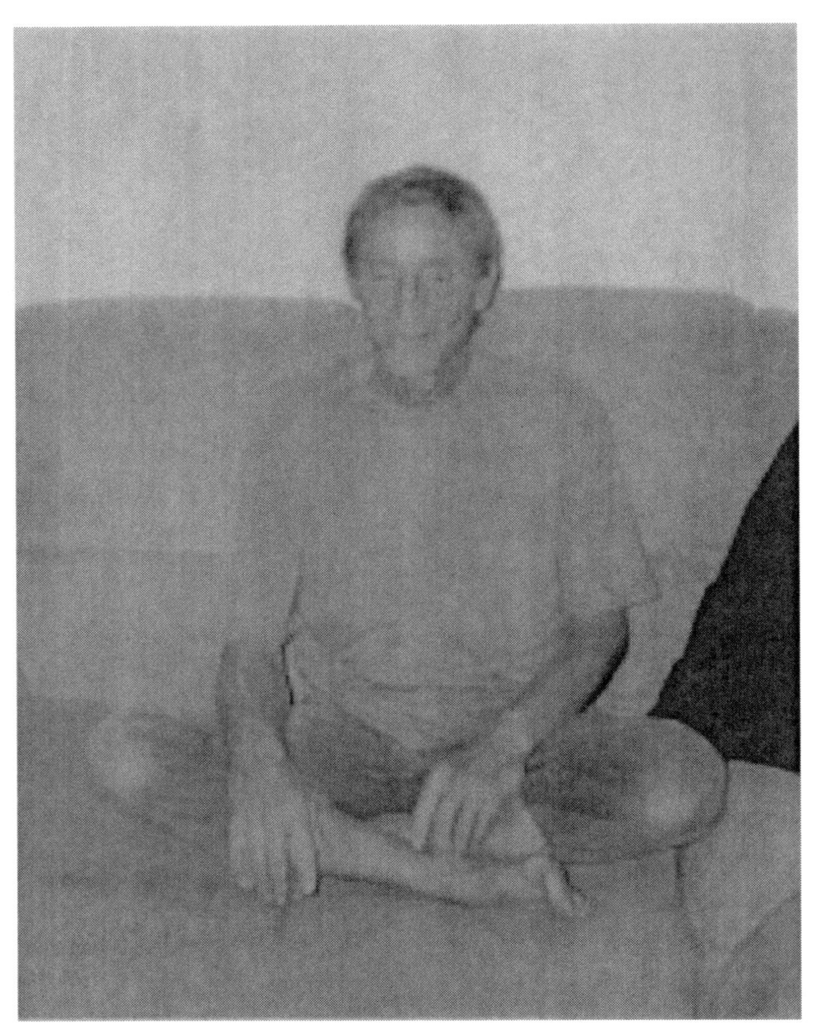

Nahshon

An Old-Time Healer

AN OLD-TIME HEALER

A true story, of a person telling a true story.
Time and place: Cafe Central, Abadiania, Brasil
                              9 November 2009
Every Day Heroes Cycle

I met him in a small cafe
Next to a spiritual hospital
In South America.

Just another client
Of the spirits there, I thought,
As we sat to hear the troubles
Of a mutual friend.

My evening had gone
As far from my agenda
As an evening generally can.

The two people I had come there to see
For respective reasons,
Had spoken together
At the next table instead –

Then somehow left this tiny cafe
Without my catching either one of them!

"Well that's Brazil," I said to myself,
Then sat and frowned,

Waiting for whatever else
Was sure to happen instead.

Only my friend sharing his problems
Kept me sitting there
Until the main event:

Our hero, next arrived, turned out to be
An Israeli, lately from San Francisco.
And when our mutual friend left,
He began to speak.

"I was at a healing place
Of some sort long ago," he said,
"And as I was about to leave
I saw a woman in great distress.

"Something in me knew her
From the past somehow,
And I had to help her then."

Minutes earlier, discussing healing paradigms,
I had mentioned an old one,
Not at all in fashion today:

Cued by some reference to shamanism,
I had mentioned those
Who take on another's illness,
And then somehow must heal themselves.

Now he continued:
"I said that <u>only</u> if it was necessary,
<u>Only</u> lacking any other way,
I would take on her disease myself
So that she could heal."

His offer was accepted, it seems,
By an unhappy spirit,
Whose invasion of the woman's body
Had made her ill.

So here sat my new friend,
Long since informed
Of the woman's full recovery;

While he, quite the mystery
To his doctors these 25 years,
Sleeps not at all –
His autonomic system
Quite off line, he says.

A spiritual pilgrim even before
His great sacrifice,
Now he faces quite a conundrum:

The invading soul, you see,
Is with him by invitation –
Spoken aloud for the sake of
A love dimly remembered!

Patient all these years, now he has come
To the sort of a healing place
Where they will remove that one –
But only in a very gentle way.

                 KYD
                 10 November 2009
                 Abadiania, Brasil

VANISHING BUFFALO

A true story.
Time and place: At a spiritual hospital
                  22 and 25 November 2009
Wide, Weird, Wonderful World Cycle

Those old time buffaloes sure were tough —
At least in the days of the great white hunters.

I mean like if some fool
With a slow action rifle
Would come out and start shooting —

They just stood there!

That's the story I heard anyway —
And half of what I think I've learned
Is from stories like that.

They were so spiritual —
"In total acceptance" said the storyteller —
I mean really radical man!

So I got a guy to make me
A little wooden buffalo
To wear around my neck.

This was way cool.
I didn't need no shaman
To tell me
What my totem would be.

Now I'll use shamans when they're around –
Which ain't very often –
But more often I end up wingin' it.

So here I was goin' along
Wearin' my buffalo for a few years.

And one day I was
Sittin' at a holy place.
Having a day of silence,
Half through writing a poem –

When a guy caught sight of me.

Now you'd have to know this guy!
Maybe he was one of those
Old time buffalo hunters
 (In one of those past lives
That we don't talk about much.)

That day he bagged me anyway.

Well this guy has a disability certainly.
And he needs the help many of us give him,
To get to places around the neighborhood,

But just like the Old Days,
If he needs one buffalo
He'll go ahead and shoot several.

And if he needs a few minutes of my time,
He doesn't mind taking an hour or two.

I went over when he called
And showed him the little note I carry:
"I am not talking today."
In three languages actually.

He was familiar with my practice
Of silent days,
And asked for a ride
On the back of my bicycle,
To a café three blocks away.

We had done it the week before,
And I nodded agreement –
Reckoning to be back to my writing
In a few minutes.

Well he goes to that café every Sunday,
And knows exactly when they open.
He had the advantage on me there.

Walking toward the bicycle parking,
He stopped to chat for half an hour
With a woman
Who had said hello to him once.

So I sat smiling and nodding,
Reminding myself of my buffalo dharma –
And only then did I learn from their talk
That it was more than an hour
 'Til the café would open.

Having no place at the café
To sit and wait to get in,
He was planning to kill an hour more
Of my time along the way.

As he walked the next 30 yards,
I went and brought the bicycle over,
While he busied himself
Developing his next delay.

No place here to buy
A bottle of water, he mused.
But how about some padding
For the seat, then –

Could we find someone to give him some?

Still having no means
On this day of silence
To call him on his tricks,
I watched silently.

Then suddenly it happened:

I looked down
And the buffalo was missing
From its cord around my neck!

Hooked securely,
Neither accident nor theft
Could be the cause.

"It's those spirit entities again,"
I thought.
So I wrote the man a note:
"I'm in the middle of a poem."
Exclamation point too.

"What's that supposed to mean," he said.

So I got on my bike
And went back to my
Favorite seat for writing.

So much for buffalo dharma today.
The only thing was
What to do next:

To buy a new buffalo — or wait
For a different totem to volunteer?

For three days
I wore that empty lanyard —
Inviting the answer to appear.

An eagle perhaps?
I had thought of that once —

An exciting image,
Soaring high in the realm of spirit!

Many other animals too
Had their great paths
To lead me on —

Hanging there
In front of my heart.

For three days I busied myself then —

Praying at that holy place
For love to fill this old heart,
With plenty left to share.

Begging daily for length of life,
To protect my partner
From the worst of her disease.

Those three days I waited.

And sat finally
In the spiritual current room
For healing practice with the group –

On a day when a few flowers were blessed,
Then given out, like many days before –

Seemingly at random, one might think,
Though never one for me.

Eyes closed, as was the custom there,
I attended to
The little spiritual work I know,

When suddenly in my lap,
Something thorny did appear.

Peeking ever so slightly
There I saw it!

A rose.

A few moments I reflected
Then cried out in my heart:
Wait a minute!
Spreading love around.
Protecting someone.
That's what roses do!

No need for any other totem
To soar around the sky.

The rose itself is totem
Enough for the likes of me!

So even now, before
I could find a rose figure
To hang there on that cord,

Already it speaks up many times —

Softening a feeling.
Refining a thought.

And now a loving friend
Is seeking out a rosy image
To hang upon that cord,

And it will be complete.

KYD
2009
Abadiania, Brasil

CONFESSION

A true story.
Time and place: Near a holy place
                  Abadiania, Brasil
                  October and November 2009
Wide, Weird, Wonderful World Cycle

What would it take
To tell all my stuff,
All my ugly little secrets,
To one other person?

To be relieved once and for all,
Of the burden of carrying
All those things in a big old bag,
That God sees through anyway?

In twenty some years in recovery groups
Always I had stopped short of that moment –
Where we open the bag,
And show it all to someone.

Yes it would be such a relief
Once the act was done,
A whole new world ahead
When finally that step was taken!

But my pride,
That great organ of shame,
Stood always in the way –

Twenty two years at a standstill.
Then suddenly the visitations started!

Two old friends showed up
To break me loose from this.

Not an easier way through –
I could not call it that –
But simply one that I would not refuse.

What cast of characters, you ask?
Yes, we can speak of that:

Sitting at a table
By my solitary house,
In a hidden spot
With seating just for three –
Suddenly I was no more alone.

Old friends they were –
Yet unlike when I knew them once!

One a sweet and loving soul
Who gently turned down my proposal
Nearly 30 years before —
Then died a few years later on.

The other, big and strong and lesbian,
A co-worker when we met
In the mental health services field —

And she had died
Just earlier in the year.

We sat at my little table
From that day —

They to hear my little tales of woe —
And able only, I am told,
To *smell* the food and drink before us.

I to guess
What might their answers be —
And put them to the test
With good results.

And so communing thus,
With old friends who seemed,
By all my little senses,
To get nothing in the trade —

EVERY DAY HEROES

I began, as days passed,
To feel myself quite selfish;

And convicted of that, soon was
Reminded of all the other secret faults,
Held tightly under wraps
These many years.

So what should happen next!

From somewhere came the idea,
Much too wise in its simplicity
To be my own —

That here were two
Who loved me in their way;

A way in which,
Knowing all that I did
And most of what I thought,
Still they loved me just the same.

And here was I,
Scared all these years
Of exposure to the light,
Since none could love me then!

But with me sat my two old friends —
To hear all the worst about myself,

While they, inured
To the bright lights of spirit life,
Would see me no worse
Than they already could.

<u>Such</u> <u>a</u> <u>deal</u>!

I spoke freely then,
Of cruelties and thoughtless acts,
Of friends let down and trusts betrayed.

All the haunting memories
Of a long life
With its ups and downs.

And 'though I can not see these two
In what I call a usual sense –
Still I could feel that day
The great smiles upon their faces;

As I lay down before them
A burden so heavy
That my shoulders had begun to ache.

KYD
22 November 2009
Casa de Dom Inacio, Brasil

CALIBRATING HER

A true story of a trap that worked.
Time and place: Fruitty's in Abadiania
                  1 October 2010
Goofy Poet's Cycle

"Gotcha!" I hollered to myself,
Gloating openly in my mind.

She was in a slight frenzy
For a moment or two,

And seemed not even to hear
As I said to her out loud
"This has been a test."

Never mind.
I'll tell her that
And lots more too,
The next time that we talk.

She believes – and somehow
May have been taught –
That she's of little worth.

Sad stories she has
To tell from her life;

And in them
Each begins and ends
With an apology,
For burdening the listener so.

Never mind that I want my friends
To release what must come out.

If there's no perfect façade
To present to the world,
Of a happy and seamless life,

Then manners from
Where she grew up

Will have her say
Nothing at all.

Well have it as you will then
You families from
A cold and distant time.

But soon came the day
When she came to me,
"Mea culpas" at the max.

Her ancient etiquette
Holding her back no more,
A few stories
She was ready to tell —

Although surely someone
Would then swat her down,
For feelings in disarray.

Later came the test,
That gotcha moment,
As we settled up a tab.

Some bit of proof to defend her
I must have,
When she told of her little worth!

Responding to an inner prompt,
Earlier I had said

That I would pay
For the dinner we had planned.

She brushed me off of course –
No one should pay for her –

Then ate half her dinner
And two expensive desserts.

Seeming unfazed by money wasted,
She was about to pay for her meal,

When I jumped up with a reminder
That I had said I would pay.

Such a change in her then
I wish I had filmed!
Repenting the junk that she ate.

Too polite to refuse as I stood there
With money in my hand,

Her waste seemed now a disaster
When paid by someone else.

Now what do you think will happen next
When she tells of her little worth,

Of how patient I am
With the burden she claims to be?

She's been calibrated now!!
Before witnesses no less –

An avid people watcher
On the balcony above,

Who coached her on the spot
How better to respond to the treat;

And a friend who owns the place,
Who was ringing up the meal.

She cared more now
For the money wasted,
As two witnesses can attest,

Than had it been at her own expense
As she thought when she ordered up.

Gotcha!!

                    KYD
                    2 Oct 2010
                    Abadiania, Brasil

THEN CAME JOANNA

This is a true story.
Time and place: Near the Casa de Dom Inacio,
                  Abadiania
                  Christmas season 2010
Every Day Heroes Cycle

A big strong man, ascended already
In the art of breaking up fights,
Was the first to try his hand,

As a mother and her son
Came to blows
In the middle of a street.

But all to no avail,
And still the two went at it.

Then came JoAnna,
Skinny and ill.

Tormented in the head
By spirits angry and distraught,

Tormented in the gut
By tiny beings run amuck
For longer than she could stand.

There came JoAnna
To the middle of that street –

With words of peace,
And reconciliation long practiced
In those struggles in her head.

With wise and simple counsel
Of how to put it all to rest.

And in such a struggle as this –
Mother and son come to blows –

It took this sensitive woman
With combat experience of her own

To point in the direction of peace
And to prove in subtle ways

That love can walk with us
Wherever we are,
And put the heart to rest.

KYD
1 Jan 2011
Abadiania, Brasil

THE MAN WHO PREVENTED WORLD WAR THREE

A true story, subject to interpretation.
Time and place: San Francisco Bay Area, 1980s
Every Day Heroes Cycle

Lee dropped out.

He quit his job at the brokerage house,
And became the strange man down the block
Whom all the children loved to visit.

His wife said it happened after an acid trip,
But Lee never spoke about that.

Actually he didn't speak very much
About anything, most of the time.

Lee left his previous wife,
And married a disabled woman
With a gift for astrology,
Who loved him with all her heart.

In fact she sat across the street from his house
Until he left the other woman
And came to her.

Lee's parents didn't like any of this.
They were planning their deaths,
And had an entirely different life in mind for him.

"We'll give him part of his inheritance now," they said.
"The responsibility will snap him out of this."

Lee had had no savings left –
If ever he had any.

Meanwhile, psychics were predicting
World War Three
Would be started over Biafara.

Then news broke out
Of the famine there.

"Send in your money!" the television cried.
"People are dying as we speak."

Lee sent in his thirty thousand dollars;
His sister was appointed executor of the will,
To give Lee a little money at a time;
And we never had that war.

Of what he had,
I think Lee gave the most.

That's my friend Lee –
The man who prevented World War Three.

KYD
28 May 2004
Casa de Dom Inacio, Brasil

LOVE LETTER TO THE ANGEL NADIA

The author offers this as a true story, with no apologies
for the parts which may not be verifiable by the five
senses.
Time and place: (1) Berkeley and Eugene in the
1980s (2) Subtle realm, within hailing distance
of Pennsylvania, approx. 1998
Crazy Love Cycle

DEAR NADIA,

Do you remember when we drove out
To sit across the street from Lee's place?

Of course you do.

I don't remember whether it was
Before or after that
That I proposed to you.

Yes, I did know that you would turn me down.
It was sort of for the record, so to speak.
Or for another lifetime, perhaps.

So of course I drove you out there.
With you in front of me —
What else could I do?

You, who had the courage to enter a lifetime
With not one but three disabilities.

I know a bit of good karma when I see it!

Lee came out of that house,
And left his wife,
And married you.

Lee, paradoxical figure,
Unknown hero,
On an eccentric spiritual path I know nothing of.

You made the wise and heartful choice –
Then gave me an additional karmic opportunity:
To perform your wedding,
On that footbridge over the river.

If I see you in Heaven,
It will be you who helped me get there.

Do you remember the times
You startled me with your purity?

I used to think purity was foolishness,
'Til I saw the real thing in you.

I remember when I heard of your death.
Lee says the baby cried,

And he got up
And brought her to you
And found you dead.

You predicted your own death –
My best and only astrology student,

The thing that worried you, you told me,
Was that your parents would
Take the child from Lee.

They did, too.
And I never thought of a way to prevent it.

I asked to go and visit your parents once –
Hoping to see the child.
But your father said no.

You have done better by me.

Numerous times you have shown up.
I don't know how many lines of my poetry
Are actually your lines.

You blew your cover, though.
Remember that time
You spoke to me through my teacher?

Well, she saw your wings!
When I get to Heaven,
I will know you from a distance.

KYD, 30 May 2004
Abadiania, Brasil

ROWDY LOVE

A true story.
Time and place: A few years of my life
                  Through June 2009
Crazy Love Cycle

"If the angel of death comes for me
I will fight."

That's what I told the God
Who loves me so well.

"You have honored me
By letting me be here at all.

"Your kindness and mercy
In letting me be with my beloved Gemini
Exceeds anything I have seen.

"But now a disease process
Threatens her with indignities
At the end of life,
Which I can never stand by
And watch from over there."

Already in the latter part
Of a lifetime
Full of past life karma
Well deserved —

What was I to dread now?
A different sort of karma, perhaps?

A poetically perfect consequence,
Earned here by my love
Too passionate to let her have
Whatever lesson that was hers.

"A mere change of pace,"
I counseled myself then.

"To live quite a loveless life,
Then cap it off by loving too much –
That ain't bad," I thought.

"Next after that
An actual sanity will come!
Let me see the karma
That one rides in on."

But actually, you know,
My belief system
Set me up for it!

Not bent nor schooled
To the ways of the crusades –

Owner of no wrathful God –

I got no picture of being
Swatted down in some horrible way
For my unruly love.

And so, as much curious as anxious,
I waited now to see the fruits
Of this adolescent love
In my sixties.

Would that great and mysterious God
Step on me,
As I drew my foolhardy line in the sand?

Or by some mercy inconceivable –
Even to me, who drew on it so often –
Would I see that death angel stop?

Diagnosed earlier with a cancer,
Since gone
Better and worse by turns –

Now I asked only for time
To care for my Gemini,
In ways respectful of
Each peculiarity that's in her.

If her body can be touched
In only certain ways,
Her laundry handled in a certain way
Not defensible by reason –

"Obsessive-compulsive" they call it –

And if service by a caretaker
In disregard of that
Would be to her
Unthinkable slime –

"Then let me watch with her
Those few years
And spare her that!"
That was what I cried out to God.

Then somehow the craziness in me
Said "No! Make that no request.
Stand there and tell that God
You will have it no other way!"

"If that death angel comes for me
I will fight."

That's what I heard myself saying –
And repeating for a few years.

The cancer continued
With its little ups and downs.

Still the angel paused.

Nothing in life stands still,
Of course.

My character,
Like yours and yours and yours,
Forms and reforms itself all the time.

So where then was mine to go?

Living in a defiant and pushy way
Toward my very God,

Would I become at the same time
Gentler or rougher
With that human I love the most?

You guessed it.
And so it went
For a few years more.

My beloved Gemini,
Patient with me always,
Was slow to tell me
Of the changes obvious to see.

Spiritual growth is when
I see into myself,
Then take a step ahead.

But what a mysterious
And horrible realization
This one was to be!

YES; by my bizarre heroics
I might actually keep this body alive.

In certain ways,
At certain moments,
We can get pushy with even God –
And for the little that we see,
May actually seem to prevail.

God has not the burden of ego
So easily seen in myself.

But NO, came the stunning realization –
By the very same act of pushiness
I made myself unfit for the job itself!
Here's how I found out:

I was sitting around
My mother's house, as she,
In a terminal way and aware of it,
Drew closer to Heaven,
And so radiated more loving care.

Then one day
In her charitable way
She said to stop mowing the lawn —
So that she could have a neighbor
Do it for pay.

He needed the money, she said.
For a house he was buying in Florida.
I criticized her judgment,
Reminded her of all the time on my hands,
And kept my mowing chore.

In a day or so I had a similar go 'round
With my Gemini by phone.

She showed me the similarity
Between our quarrel and my
Treatment of my mother —
And I was busted!

What a jarring turnaround it was.
My resolve turned up to the max —

Ready for years, at a moment's notice,
To fight even that fearsome angel —

Then suddenly to admit,
My plan had failed already.

Merely to prepare to fight
Was enough to lose it all!

Quickly I admitted that
My battle plan itself
Was undoing me,
As the helper that I planned to be.

For a week more, still
The loving spirits waited,
Consoling me,
As I cried each day –

Able only after that full week
To force this mouth to say:

"No Lord,
I will not fight that angel."

It's not a badge that I was seeking,
For stupid heroics!
My goal at the outset
Was to aid and comfort my lover.

Whatever would not work,
Be it ever so desperate or heartful,
Had no place in my crusade.

All that would be left
Was to satisfy the cancer –
To learn any of its lessons whatsoever –

Not to be that crab that clings;

Not to fight
When love would do as well;

Such a turnaround to make in later years!

Only then,
My inquiries have suggested,
Would the cancer go away.

This was shaping up
To be more difficult somehow
Than fighting with an angel!

KYD
8 November 2009
and previous days
Casa de Dom Inacio and nearby
Brasil

DEATH ANGEL

A true story.
Time and place: Late months of 2009 with flashbacks
Goofy Poet's Cycle

Once upon a time
A very long time ago –
Nearly half a year in fact,

I surrendered to that God
Who shows us when to come
And when to leave here.

Earlier on I had resolved,
All goofy and poetic,
That I absolutely would care for my lover
As her health condition progressed
Toward helplessness,
Before it would let her go.

I had said often that I would fight
Even that grim angel of death –
Made famous by the church
Which cares for our souls –
If he should try to take me first.

EVERY DAY HEROES

Fighting for the right
To do a loving act
Turned out to be an oxymoron, however —
As a calmer mind
Would not have needed to be shown.

And so left standing,
All armored up
With no place to fight,

Battered and bruised
By nothing at all,

Soon I retreated to a tiny house
By a mighty healing center.

I felt at first no healing process,
Nothing to resemble what I would need
To go the distance with my fervent chore,
Of healing without a fight.

And so I cried out —
To friends Over There,
Those who comfort me
And care for me
No matter what.

Well one of those, I always knew,
Was an angel once incarnate –
A loving earthly friend in Berkeley days.

So often in the background
When help was needed –
Hard to catch at her loving acts –

This time she showed up first,
As near as I could tell;

And with another friend of mine in tow,
Who had crossed over only months before.

Now she watched with me every day:

Patching up my battered spirit –
Coaching me to earn properly
The release from my own disease –

Even interceding for me,
As I pleaded to the healing entities there.

Then finally I got it.
The angel thing!

If I were that loving God,
Boundless in my wisdom and compassion,
Whom would I send
To bring a dear one home?

Would I send that dreadful caricature
Painted in churchly art,
To carry a soul to paradise?

Well, no!
Answering my own survey,
My little opinion poll –

I would search out that angel
Who loved the person most,
The one who understood him best;

And that angel,
That best qualified one,
I would send not to bag him
And drag him home.

But rather to reveal the choices
On this planet of free will.

And so it has been.

My angel of death,
I realize now,
Was to be *my beloved Nadia!*

The one whom I proposed to once.
The one to whom I wrote
A love letter poem
Years after her death.

No use messing with God.
He/She had me coming and going.

Had I persisted in my bravado —
Had I charged forth one day
To fight that angel of death —

Still there would have been no fight.
Never could have been a fight.

KYD
16 November 2009
Abadiania, Brasil

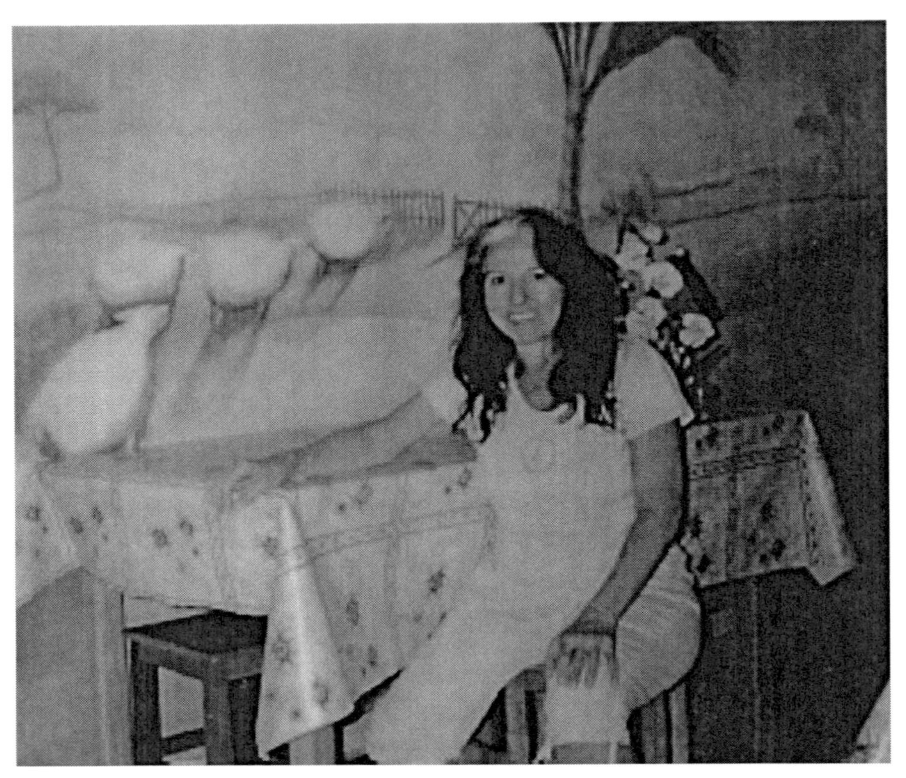

Jean-Marie

SILENCE OF A POET

A true story.
Time and place: With a disabled mother.
                  En route to Brasilia airport
                  6 March 2006; and previous week
Crazy Love Cycle

Unreasonably and against all odds
You cared for your child;
And unreasonably well he thrived.

You told me of the miracles required of you
In order to do that –
And I began to sit at your feet.

You told me of your cats,
And how you care for them –
And I began to bring you presents.

You loved the flower
That you carried with you today,
And shared your drinking water with it.

And I could only wait and watch
'Til you ascended to the sky –

In an airplane, that is.

I am one of the surviving romantic poets,
And it is of you that I will sing.

                    KYD
                    6 March 2006
                    Abadiania,Brasil

LET ME SIT AT YOUR FEET AGAIN

A true story
In the form of a loving letter,
Written December 2009
Every Day Heroes Cycle

Come to Abadiania again, dear one,
Where the spirit entities are big and bold.

Where things happen always
That only the heart can know.

You who wilted
When your son turned against you —

Then came back to life
When asked to bring a rose totem
To put my life together again.

"Now I have a mission," you said,
And found a cheap flight easily.

You whose lover
Rode off with another,

And now you will walk again
To this holy place
On feet that barely work –

To seek again the signs
Of what your love can do.

You whose job as guide
Was taken away
To test you in your role –

And now move on with courage
Shining in the fore.

A guide to those you never see
Who watch you as you go.

Let me sit at your feet again
Dear one, and watch you as before.

Though I have coveted your affection,
Given to another in the world,

Still you have heard
With quiet understanding
My little tales and woe.

Let me sit at your feet again,
Busy as you are.

If I can do some little thing,
Like push you in a chair,

Then my failures with my own son
Are forgotten for a time,
And regrets return no more.

Let me sit at your feet again
To see by the light of your life,

The little things I've been stopping at
While wonders lie ahead.

Take a room in my house even,
And I will watch quietly –

No more the alarm clock to dread,
With your ironic smile
My first greeting of the day.

Let me sit at your feet again –
To tell how your example
Has gotten me through
So many of my little tests!

EVERY DAY HEROES

The troubles in your life just now
Are awesome as I hear them,

And none that I know
Has handled such a thing.

Yet somehow I,
Foolish and insensitive by turns,

Have been left somehow,
In the wisdom of the gods,
Who will have nothing from us
But greatness in the end,

To watch this place
Where you will come
For healing just in time,

By great and magical forces
To keep you on the team.

Let me sit at your feet again –
At least this one more time.

KYD
9 and 12 December 2009
Abadiania, Brasil

APPENDIX ONE:
This is Poetry?

Poetry, if my combination of meager scholarship and brash conjecture holds up at all, must have served historically to make literature memorable, during a very long epoch in which we were dependent on this planet upon oral tradition, for much or all of our historical and scholarly learning.

To my precious doubters I say: Try memorizing the lyrics of a popular song, aided by its rhyme and alliteration and meter, and then try memorizing a passage of prose, otherwise comparable, but without those catchy devices. Certain poets, even today, have been known to criticize other poets for showing up at a poetry reading event without first memorizing their work.

Living today however, with a wealth of technology, such as movable type, we have less incentive than before to depend upon those wonderful mnemonic devices aforementioned. We may stand up to read our material, or publish it in a book, and need only withstand the scorn of a few lyrical fundamentalists.

I myself enjoy an equivocal relationship to tradition. Whenever I come upon an honored tradition which has been flying beneath my radar, I don't know, until the moment I react abruptly to it, whether I will embrace it as the champion of some institution without which I would find it ever so difficult to live in our rapidly changing world; or whether I will say to it "Thank you ever so much for your good and faithful service we don't need you anymore;" or whether, even, I will tell it "Get lost. You have done nothing but get in the way."

And thus it is for me no less so with the traditional devices of poetry. I still have a poem I was assigned to write in high school. It's something about "I wish I had a dish of fish." With a start like that, it was many years until it occurred to me that I could write poetry at all – and then only after I had let go of several things which served earlier poets so well; such as rhyme and meter.

When the obvious and easily counted features of poetry have been stripped away by some risk-taking old man, however, there remain for this person some definitive characteristics of poetry, which I would not know how to do without:

1. In my work, those pieces which are formatted differently from prose are the ones which I have called poetry. (Let them rail, at the open-mic celebrations.)
2. Poetry is evocative of feelings.
3. Poetry may take the liberty (and mine generally does) of dispensing with rationalist, reductionist and/or positivist rules of evidence and proof. It's the heart that needs convincing here.
4. Trains of thought may be altered at one time abruptly and at another time gently, thus creating a sort of rhythm which draws greater attention to the poet's favorite images.
5. Less words very often are better than more.
6. A mind caressed by these devices sometimes is more ready to hear from the magical-mystical side of things.

So it is then, that I call the material in this book poetry. But poetry or prose, each account is true, and told as accurately as I am able. And that truthfulness after which I hunger and thirst is as much a faithfulness to what the heart knows and remembers as to that which the mind retains.

KYD
17 June 2007
Tulsa

APPENDIX TWO:
Recognizing An Every Day Hero

**"There is no saint without a past,
and no sinner without a future."**
–Sri Babaji

All "men" are created equal, according to the Declaration of Independence. Actually children and women are too.

If we have an end, we might all end up equal too – or at least so far "up there" as to be out of sight, way out of sight of those of us still in the habit of judging our fellow pilgrims.

So, if I attempt to make any generalizations about every day heroes as a group, it is only in order to find them and bask in their glow – never to judge them, nor to judge others by comparison.

But for the illusion of linear time, it seems, each person I pass on the street is as admirable and wonderful as the great ones we hear of. That's the theory, and I'm stickin' to it!

So here I am, relieved of the duty of condemning half the folks I meet – a duty I have performed faithfully for most of my life, and frequently still do. We're all such fine people, if only one will look deeply enough – yourself included, dear reader. But having said this, still I have offered not so many clues how to find and describe those glorious and elusive perpetrators of every day heroism that I so love to write about.

WHERE TO BEGIN

Let me offer a parallel example, and maybe this will help: I talk to the angels every day. I have been doing this for many years. And lately I actually pick up the answers around me, to some of the questions I have asked them.

Now how do I do that? If I could explain any of that, maybe I actually would. But I know one thing that's been necessary: *I believe they exist.* I look for the signs of the angelic presence all around me. I never tire of watching for that.

So what about spotting the every day heroes, and the signs of their presence? This is not rocket science. I have learned to think of them as being all over the place! (They are every one of us actually, although some of us may still be more in disguise than others.)

And thinking that way, in my own experience at least, I got better at noticing when sweet and beautiful things happened around me. After that, I managed to form the habit of quickly looking around to see: *who did that?*

HOW TO SPOT THEM

1. Suppose something unkind is done to someone, and immediately I watch for the sparks to fly. I saw what happened. I know how I would react to that. But strangely the sparks don't come! Something has happened here. If you're looking for every day heroes, you may just have seen one. Go check 'em out!

2. Suppose someone needs a bit of help, a volunteer so to speak. Now watch and see if someone volunteers a little too quickly. She or he has formed a habit of helping out when needed — no thinking time required, it's automatic.

'Better check it out, see what kind of person would live like that.

3. Did someone take what seemed like a big risk, to help or protect another person? Maybe even to help an animal in need? 'Some unreasonable act of crazy love. Maybe they'll get fired for it or something; but usually the act itself turns out well. 'A loving and compassionate act that no one can call reasonable. There's an obvious every day hero. Keep your eye on him or her. Sooner or later they'll do it again.

PHENOMENA OF EVERY DAY HEROES

There is, down deep inside of every one of us, a knowledge of what's right; also the courage to act on it. That knowing, and that urge to act on it, can never be taken away—although they can be covered over ever so deeply by training or experience antagonistic to them.

That is to say, the hero hidden in anyone may break loose at any time. We might even incite folks to it now and then: "I really admired the way . . ." "When that sort of thing happens, wouldn't it be great if someone who was there would just . . .?" "If we're doin' the right thing, it doesn't really matter if some people think we're nuts." "When we do something really right on, a protection comes to us. Heaven cries out."

And once that shy little hero does get loose a time or two, the experience is such a sweet and moving one, that probably it will get loose again. An unreasonably beautiful or heartful life is such a joyful one that, once having tasted it, the person may never be counted on not to taste it again.

Could it have been thoughts of something like this that prompted the father of Siddhartha Gotthama, the Buddha, to try to keep his son sheltered from seeing all the loving and help that was needed in the world? He had heard of his son's destiny, and must have sensed that the first taste was what would get him. (He could not outmaneuver the angels, of course, and no amount of parental training and controlled experiences was able to keep the Buddha from being the Buddha.)

AND AS FOR US
   We'll see it when we believe it!

KYD
27 January 2008
Tulsa

APPENDIX THREE

THE BEATITUDES
(From the Bible, Matthew 5: 3 to 12)

Blessed are the poor in spirit: for theirs is the kingdom of heaven.

Blessed are they that mourn: for they shall be comforted.

Blessed are the meek: for they shall inherit the earth.

Blessed are they which do hunger and thirst after righteousness: for they shall be filled.

Blessed are the merciful: for they shall obtain mercy.

Blessed are the pure in heart: for they shall see God.

Blessed are the peacemakers: for they shall be called the children of God.

Blessed are they which are persecuted for righteousness' sake: for theirs is the kingdom of heaven.

Blessed are ye, when men shall revile you, and persecute you, and shall say all manner of evil against you falsely, for my sake.

Rejoice, and be exceeding glad: for great is your reward in heaven: for so persecuted they the prophets which were before you.

ABOUT THE AUTHOR

Only in his adult years has Karma Yeshe Dorje taken to visiting his poetic world. And only by some effort has he learned the way. Sometimes he comes back with a poem, always with a blessing.

The angels who go about with Yeshe are extremely forgiving. He stole his three-year-old son from the child's mother, squandered money he didn't even have on tuition while others were starving, and drank addictively for nearly 20 years. And still they whisper in his ear.

Yeshe has no explanation to offer for the relationship of the angels with himself as he writes. He does not think of himself as channeling his poetry – unless channeling is something that most poets do. But the best poems seem somehow to be theirs.

As a stubborn spiritual seeker (oxymoron acknowledged) and improvident father, Yeshe has indulged his curiosity and love of variety by working as a cab driver in New York, a hippie bus driver (Green Tortoise) on the West Coast, a paratransit driver, a welfare case worker in New York, a concrete construction worker in a Middle Eastern country, a wheelchair ramp builder in Berkeley, a rehabilitation technician, a youth director in a Puerto Rican church in New Jersey, an astrology teacher (unpaid), a living skills instructor, the classification officer in a reformatory, a rehabilitation plan writer, a newspaper reporter in the Princeton area, a case manager in the developmental disabilities field, an adaptive travel professional, a job coach at a recycling center, a lift-gate van operator in wilderness outings, an emergency transportation coordinator, a residential assistant in a shelter in the mental health field, a guide for those visiting a Spiritist healing center, and a special education school bus driver. Yeshe completed a counseling internship in a "troubled" high school in New Jersey, and a practice teaching assignment in English as a second language at a Chinese community center in California.

Yeshe believes that he has learned more at the places he has worked than in the universities he attended. He does however hold a B.A. degree; plus certificates in Spanish and in teaching English as a second language (TESL). He also has dropped out of five very nice graduate schools, a theological seminary, an institute for Oriental medicine, and a psychic institute. Yeshe completed a brief apprenticeship in Japanese temple building carpentry.

Yeshe grew up in Stewartsville, New Jersey, under the birth name Ray Churchfield, Jr., and later received his present name from Kalu, Rinpoche, a Tibetan teacher.

As a fancier of languages, Yeshe has learned a tolerable skill in German from classes, in Portuguese by spending time in Brasil, and in Spanish partly from classes and partly from immersion. He travels when he has money to do so.

Religiously Yeshe is a world citizen. He is a Buddhist when he is with the Buddhists, a Christian when he is with the Christians, and a Spiritist when he is with the Spiritists. His love of paradoxes serves him well here.

Yeshe knows very little about computers, sings out of tune, and was unreliable in love relationships most of his adult life.

Yeshe maintains, in the face of all this, that if his poetry is any good he may still get into Heaven.

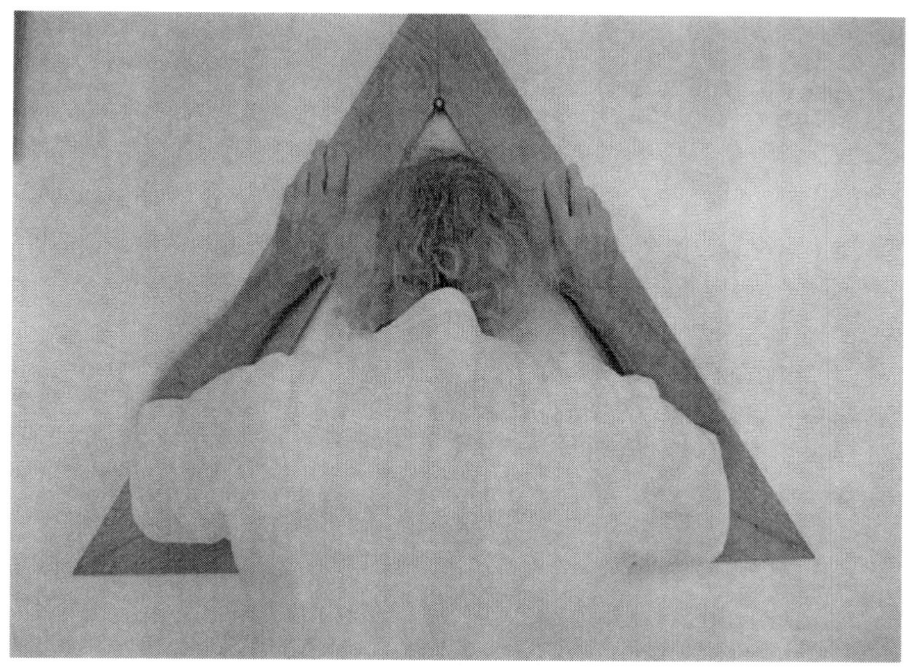

The author, seen here consulting the

spirit entities at a spiritual

hospital, hopes for each and every

reader to find one more every day hero

-- the one in their own heart.

WHAT THE CRITICS SAY ABOUT "EVERY DAY HEROES"

Yeshe Dorje is this angelic looking person with a hint of smile in his outlook, carrying a considerable amount of very small, red, unexpected long carpets under his left arm.

They are invitations to his amazing way of storytelling enfolded in poems, like the ancient Greek poetry.

As these carpets are incredibly small, but of this invigorating red color, you can only track their magic if you go step by step. This is how you open your heart to the Everyday Hero stories. This is also how it is in everyday life to open your heart, to be confident that free will always will be a big light in the dark included. Try his poetry. It will give YOU words to express your own HERO/HEROINE experience.

> Heidemarie Drolak Wenger, author, psychotherapist, lecturer, seminar leader in Switzerland
> 12 December 2010

Yeshe Dorje's poems have a magical quality, very much like the man himself.

> Michael Chacko Daniels, haiku poet
> Morning in Santiniketan, Writers Workshop, Kolkata, 2010

What a writer!
From his heart to mine.
So truthful, so now,
so here, so much beauty.

I love you,...Sir,
and you too love us,
your readers.

Come with us, all
your readers, those
who are able to love
you, and your creations.

From Robert,
a fellow in word
truths.

These short stories by Yeshe have meaning and anticipation
that cause a person to say: "What would I do in a similar
situation?" The heroes in these stories may not realize they are
heroes. But Yeshe does and now we do.

Omer G. – award-winning journalist and seeker

CPSIA information can be obtained
at www.ICGtesting.com
Printed in the USA
FFOW04n0935221113
2452FF